CW01020098

VULCAN FOUNDRY LOCOMOTIVES

BUILT 1934
THE
VULCAN FOUNDRY
LIMITED
NEWTON-LE-WILLOWS
LANCASHIRE

D. S. E. GUDGIN

VULCAN FOUNDRY LOCOMOTIVES

1832 — 1956

BRADFORD BARTON

Another view of the massive Liberation 2-8-0s supplied to U.N.R.A.A. after the second World War (see pages 62/63). Originally conceived as a 2-10-0, the design had to be modified to suit the Yugoslavian Railways' curvature. Examples are still reported in service in Czechoslovakia and Yugoslavia.

 ISBN 0 85153 215 2

printed in Great Britain by H. E. Warne Ltd, London and St. Austell
for the publishers

D. BRADFORD BARTON LTD · Trethellan House · Truro · Cornwall · England

Introduction

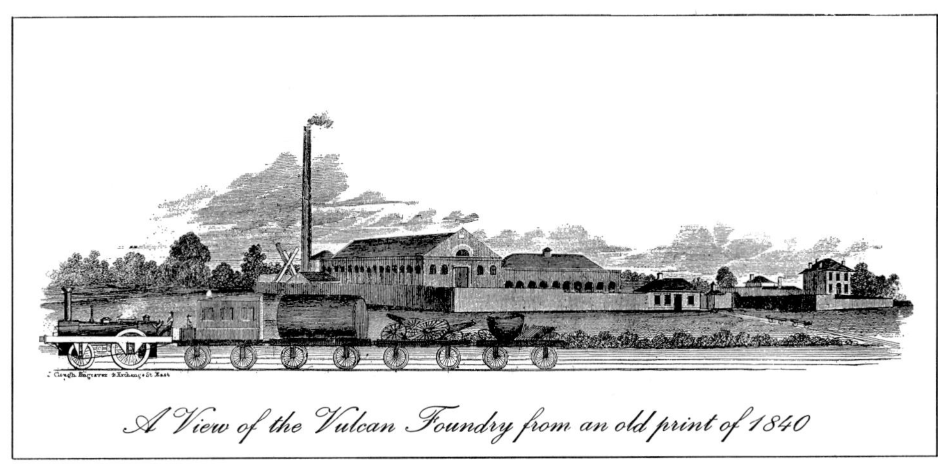

A View of the Vulcan Foundry from an old print of 1840

The Vulcan Foundry was established in collaboration with Charles Tayleur, a famous name in early locomotive engineering. The difficulties in transporting locomotives from Stephenson's Newcastle factory to Lancashire, for use on the newly opened Liverpool & Manchester Railway, were instrumental in the decision to build a new works halfway between these two cities, near Newton-le-Willows.

The first locomotive, aptly named *Tayleur*, was produced in 1832 for the North Union Railway, followed by three more for the Warrington & Newton Railway. Vulcan were soon building locomotives for various of the new railways springing up all over Britain and they were also very early in the export market. By 1840, engines had been sent to no fewer than five Continental countries and even to the U.S.A. Locomotive building continued apace and several famous locomotive engineers were connected with the Foundry, including (Sir) Daniel Gooch who completed his apprenticeship term in 1834.

William Kirtley, who subsequently became Locomotive Superintendent of the Midland Railway, was for a period in charge of the engine-house that drove the machinery at Vulcan Foundry and H. Dübs, who later founded the Glasgow works of the North British Locomotive Co, served as Works Manager, whilst the brother of Sir Daniel Gooch was General Manager from 1864 to 1897.

In 1852, the long association with India commenced and between 1852 and 1952 over 2,750 locomotives were supplied to the railways there—an average of more than one a fortnight for 100 years.

The first locomotive for Japan was delivered in 1871 and over the ensuing years many noteworthy experimental locomotives were produced at Newton-le-Willows, particularly the earlier BESA semi-standard engines for India. Output for the period 1830-1890 was approaching 1,000 locomotives, some 600 of these being for export, mainly to India.

The 1914-1918 war period saw the Works heavily involved in armament production, field guns and lighter weapons being produced in quantity together with paravanes for the Admiralty.

The great importance of the Indian Railways business now became apparent. Vulcan, together with the Consulting Engineers, began the task of designing and building a whole range of broad and metre gauge locomotives to fit all of the many state systems. These are described in the ensuing pages under the 'X' and 'Y' classes, which were built over a span of 30 years, and many of them are still in service today.

The inter-war years also produced outstanding locomotives for various African countries, particularly Nigeria and the Gold Coast; at home, early deliveries in quantity of the new Stanier types, both 4-6-0 and 2-8-0, were also made to the LMSR. Argentine and China also figured prominently in the order book but, overshadowing all these, the continuous requirements for India gave the Works a remarkably steady output during the severe depression of the early 1930s. Prior to the Second World War, Vulcan had been entrusted with prototype production of the heavy infantry tank 'Matilda' and over 3,000 of these were either built at Newton-le-Willows or by sub-contractors.

In 1943, the Government ordered a change in production to locomotives and some 400 of the Austerity 2-8-0s, based on the LMS Stanier design but with parallel boiler, were produced for the Ministry of Supply and the War Department. Torpedoes and gun mechanisms were also manufactured in quantity simultaneously.

With the cessation of hostilities and a backlog of orders, an intensely busy era began. Large contracts for India, Turkey, Argentine and various African states caused the regular labour force to rise to 3,500, and for a considerable number of years two to three locomotives a week were produced. This activity was largely sustained until 1954 when world demand, plus the encroaching diesel locomotive, caused a dramatic fall-off in orders. Vulcan management had not been idle and had already produced, in conjunction with Messrs. Frich of Denmark, some express diesel-mechanical railcars and an experimental shunter. A close working arrangement with the English Electric Co, was reached and, with the facilities of a large new erecting shop, manufacture of diesel-electric and electric locomotives began. The output gradually took over from the steam locomotive departments until 1955, when Vulcan was merged with the English Electric Company. By this time, home and overseas requirements for steam locomotives had fallen dramatically.

Following a complete reorganisation of the Works and re-tooling, full scale diesel locomotive production commenced in 1956. A large share of the British Railways Modernisation Plan diesel-electric Types 1, 2, 3, 4 and 5 came off the production lines at a rate of 120-150 per year, together with prototype a.c. electric locomotives; total production of locomotives for British Railways exceeded 900. Export orders were not neglected; Poland, Brazil, Spain, Portugal, India, East Africa and Rhodesia were amongst the customers during this period.

By 1966, orders for British Railways were largely complete; export orders had reached a new low level of intake and by 1968, coinciding with the merger of English Electric and General Electric, the decision was made to cease building mechanical parts. Diesel engines, for traction, marine and industrial purposes to the well-tried pattern of the English Electric RKV series, are now the main product.

Two views of the Vulcan Works, in the 1920s and (below) in 1947. Vulcan Halt station, on the connecting link between the Liverpool and Manchester line and the LMSR main line to the North, can be seen immediately in front of the office block. Vulcan village, built in 1820, is on the right.

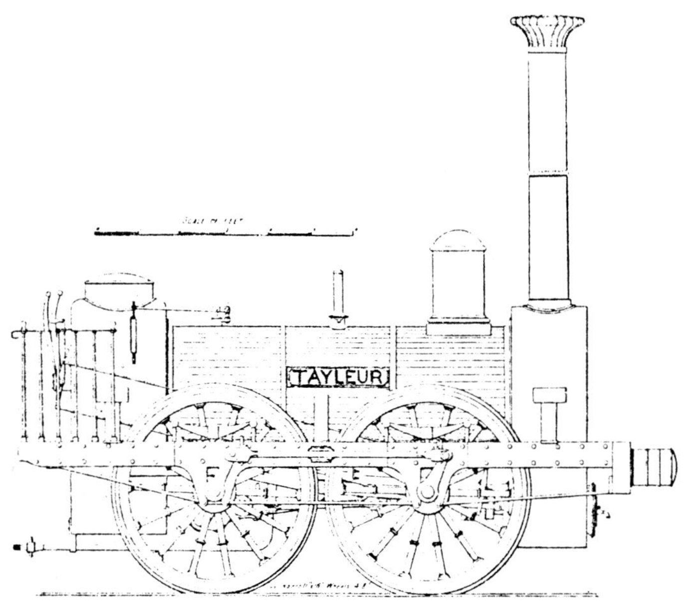

The 0-4-0 *Tayleur*, built in 1832 for the North Union Railway, was followed by three more for the Warrington & Newton Railway which traversed the west side of the Vulcan Foundry site. This locomotive was a typical Stephenson design.

Locomotive *Firefly*, built for the Camden & Woodbury Railroad (U.S.A.) in 1833, was noteworthy in that it was an example of the first bogie locomotive.

Locomotive *Titan* was built for the Liverpool & Manchester Railway. The development of coupled wheels to deal with increasing traffic on the line was becoming essential by 1834.

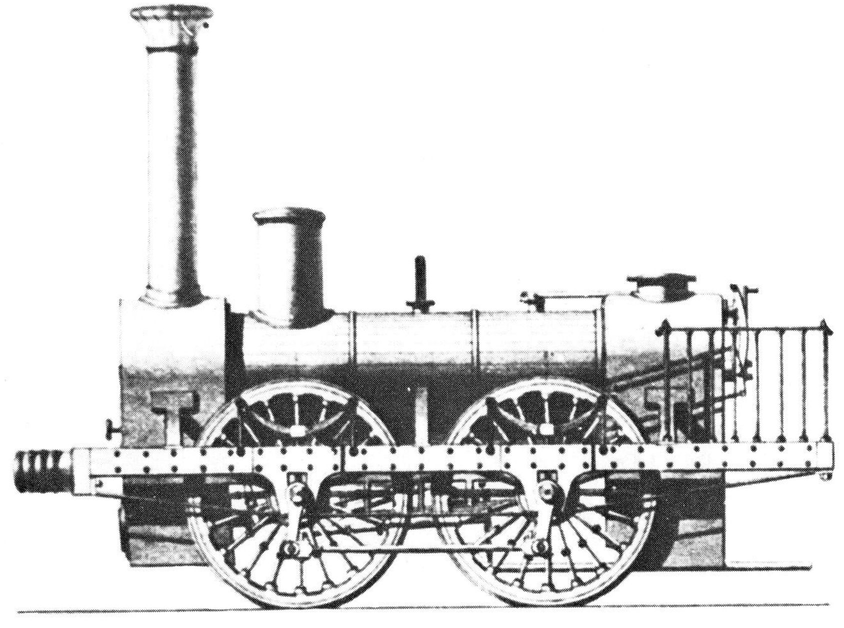

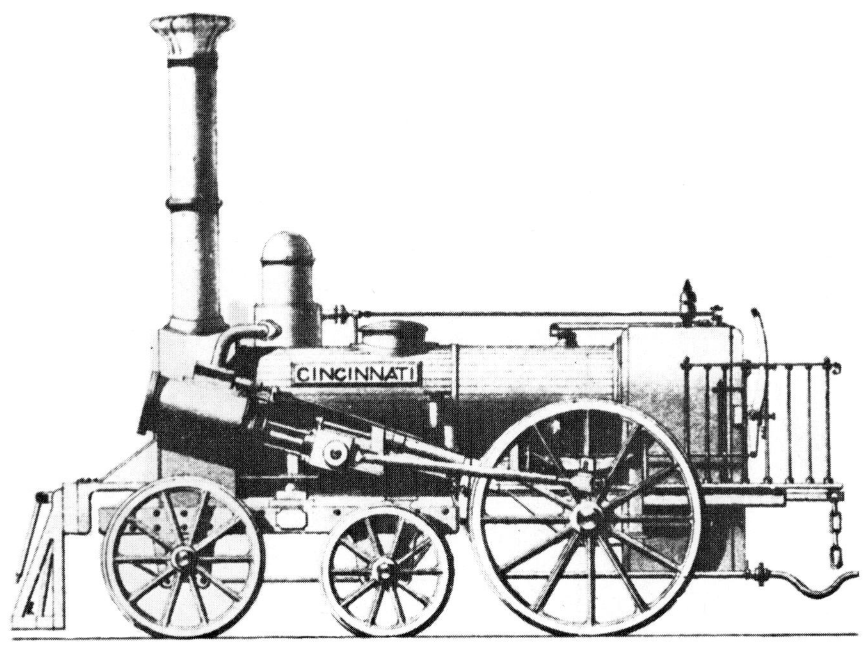

America was an early Vulcan Foundry customer; *Cincinatti*, turned out in 1835, was a bogie locomotive to deal with excessive curvature on the South Carolina Railway.

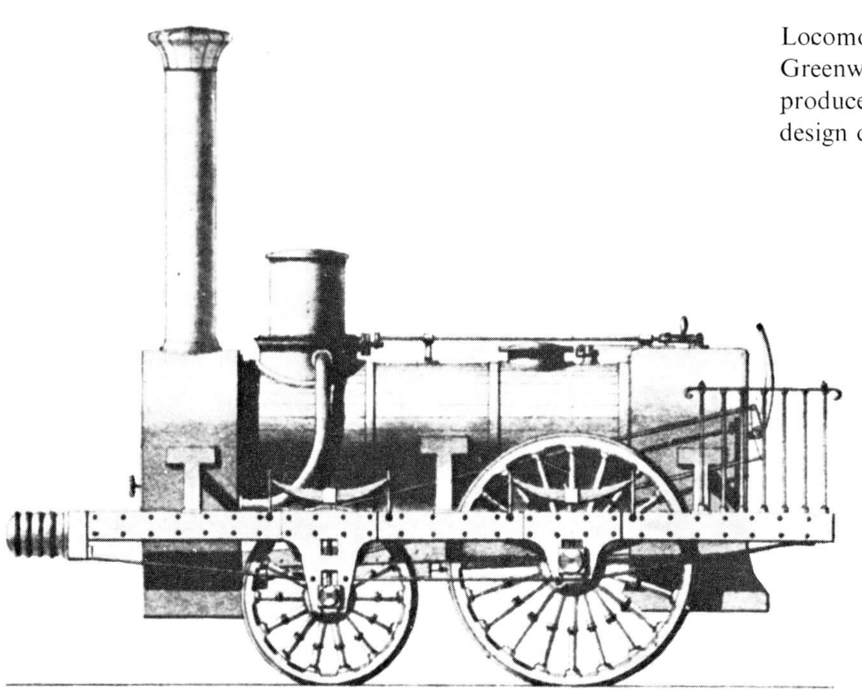

Locomotive No. 1 for the London & Greenwich Railway was the twenty-fifth to be produced at Vulcan and was of a typical design delivered in 1836.

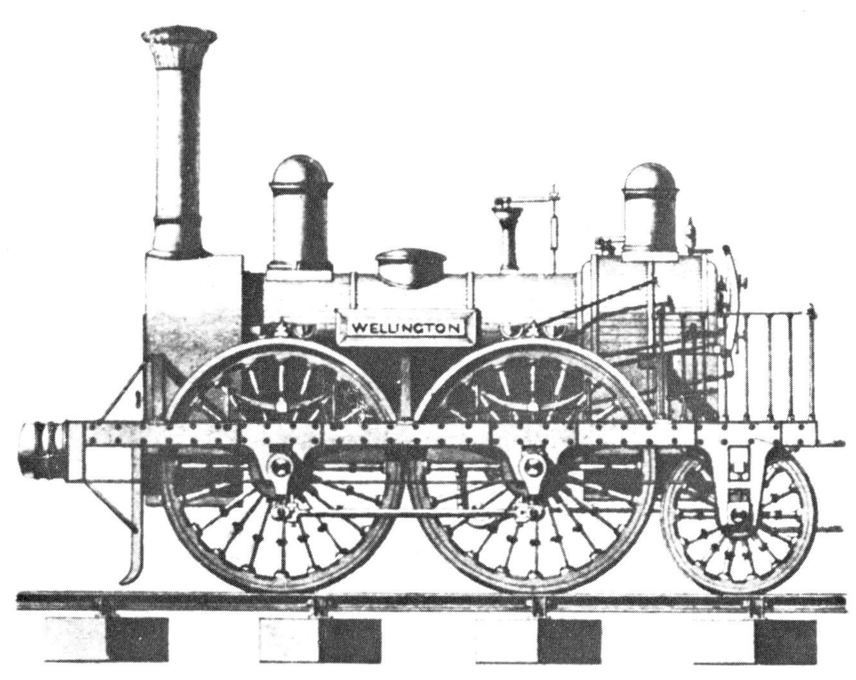

Wellington, of 1836, delivered to the order of 'Mr. Hargreaves of Bolton' for the North Union Railway, was a design that was a considerable advance in dimensions on previous machines.

No. 52 *Aeolus* was for the broad gauge Great Western Railway. Daniel Gooch had already spent a year at Vulcan Works and was about to join Isambard Kingdom Brunel. No. 52 was one of a batch of six, constructed in 1837, including one named *Vulcan*.

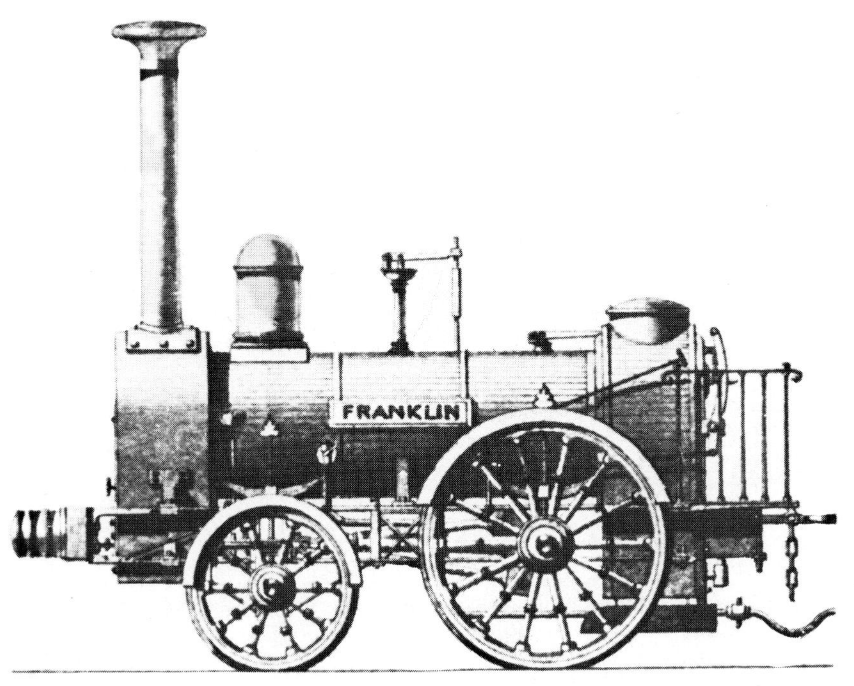

Franklin, built for the London & Birmingham Railway in 1838, was a typical small machine of the period with light bar-frame construction.

The Bristol & Birmingham Railway ordered this long-boilered machine in 1845; the design almost preceded the Crampton type locomotives.

An unusual four-coupled locomotive with jackshaft drive, produced in 1848 for the Shrewsbury & Chester Railway, was a new design of considerable advance in boiler size and was designed for goods traffic.

A 2-2-2 ordered by the Shrewsbury & Hereford Railway in 1853. Various features show a great advance on previous practice. A *Jenny Lind* similarity is apparent and the valve gear was most successful.

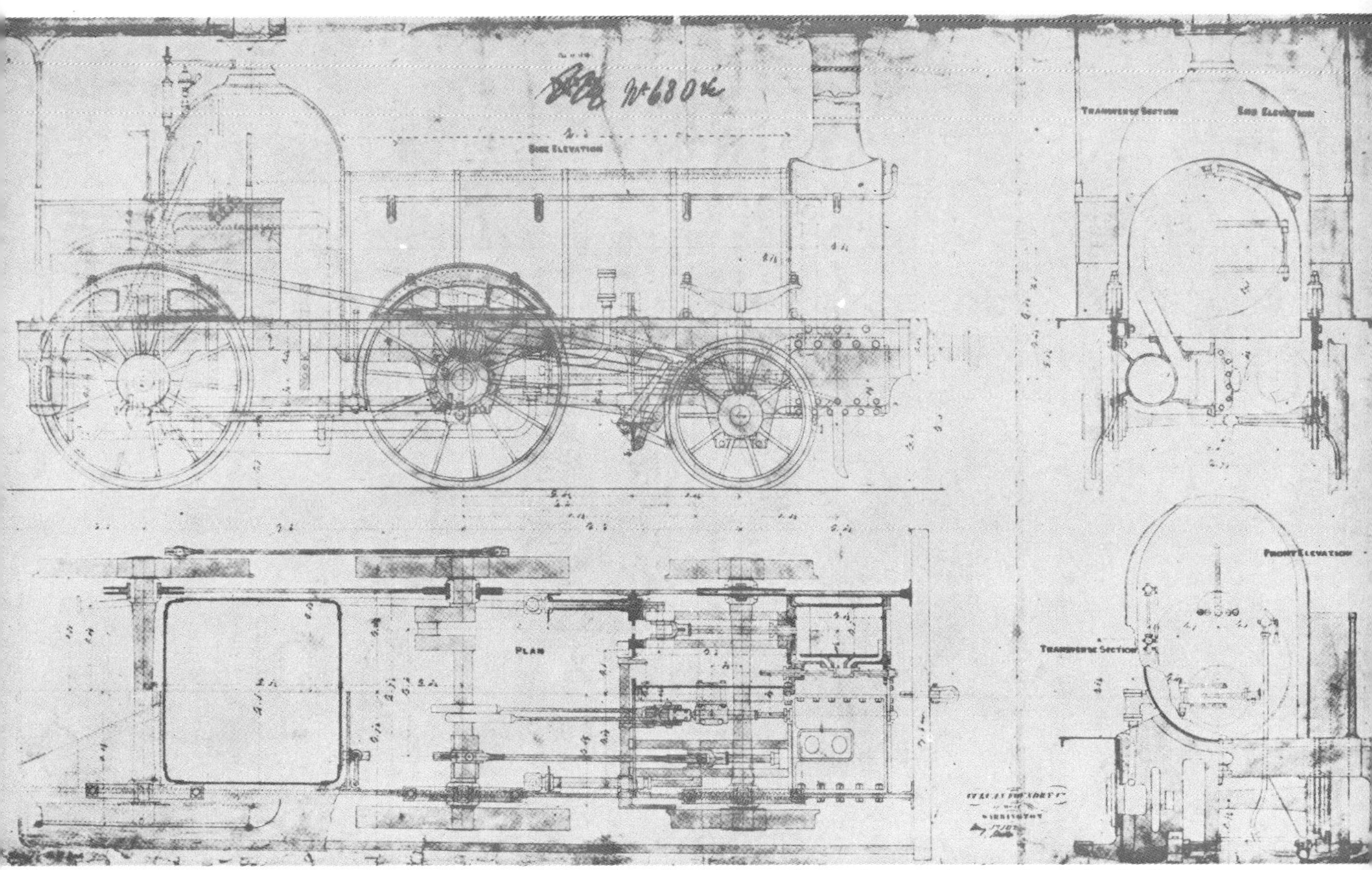

A drawing of the first main line locomotive produced for India, 1852. This was one of a batch of eight for the Bombay to Thana section of the first railway to the broad gauge, the Great Indian Peninsula. Cylinders 13in. × 20in.; coupled wheels 5ft. diameter.

merset & Dorset Railway 2-4-0 No. 23 was an early delivery in 66. The design was neat for that date and the cab unusually com-odious. Cylinders 17in. × 22in.; coupled wheels 5ft. 6in. diameter.

The Kirtley six coupled goods engine, built in 1869, was a good example of the design of the period, with cylinders 16in. × 24in. and 5ft. wheels. A boiler pressure of 130lbs per sq. in. was used. Kirtley had been employed at Vulcan Foundry in the 1830s as engineman, being in charge of a stationary engine which drove machines in the workshops.

). 461, turned out in 1866 for the Scottish North Eastern Railway. ese engines were noteworthy in that for the first time a form of ck arch was installed.

JOSEPHINE
FAIRLIE PATENT

A six-coupled heavy goods locomotive built for the Russo Konstantinofskoi Railway in 1871 for the 5ft. gauge system.

irst locomotive for the Japanese 3ft. 6in. gauge lines was deli- in 1870. In service for 59 years, this locomotive is now pre- d in a museum in Omiya. Cylinders were 12in. × 18in., coupled ls 4ft. 3in.

Zealand Railways Fairlie 0-4-4-0 *Josephine*, turned out in 1872, he forerunner of several batches. This engine is now preserved. nders 10in. × 18in.; driving wheels 3ft. 9in. diameter.

70
TALIESIN

Single Fairlie 0-6-4 tank locomotive *Snowdon Ranger* was one of a pair built for the Welsh Highland Railway. Delivered in 1875, both locomotives were deemed to be worn out in 1917 and from the serviceable parts of them appeared *Moel Tryfan*, which remained in service until 1936.

ondon, Chatham & Dover Railway (later S.E. & C.R.), ordered a batch of these 0-4-4 tank locomotives in 1875. Built for suburban work, they were fitted with reversing and condensing gear. Cylinders $17\frac{1}{2}$in. × 26in.; driving wheels 5ft. 3in.

e Fairlie 0-4-4T, designed by C. E. Spooner and Vulcan Foundry for the Ffesti- Railway. Delivered in 1876, *Taliesin* was employed on the lighter passenger trains withdrawal in 1927, having been fitted with an all-over cab. Cylinders $8\frac{1}{4}$in. × driving wheels 2ft. 8in.

One of a large class of heavy 0-8-0 tank locomotives built in 1891, for banking duty, principally on the Ghat inclines on the Great Indian Peninsula Railway. Some 85 were produced to this design, which was regarded as standard.

veral of these early standard 'F' class 0-6-0s were built for the Indian Railways etre gauge between 1875-76, many fitted for wood burning. They were stated to be le to draw loads of 600 tons at 15 mph. Cylinders were 14in. × 20in., pressure 0lbs sq. in.

nother early Indian standard, the 'O' class metre gauge passenger engine was built quantity from 1882 onwards. Wood was again the main fuel. Cylinders were in. × 20in., pressure 150lbs. sq. in.

The first 4-4-2 tank locomotive in the British Isles was one of a batch that Vulcan Foundry delivered to the Taff Vale Railway in 1888. The design was a considerable advance on existing types and the class lasted in passenger traffic until 1924.

Hull & Barnsley Railway 0-6-0 goods engine, one of a batch built in 1891 to the design of Matthew Stirling. The domeless boiler was a feature of most Hull & Barnsley locomotives. Cylinders 18in. × 26in.; coupled wheels 5ft. diameter.

5.

VULCAN LOCOMOTIVE WORKS.

FOUR CYLINDER BALANCED COMPOUND

FOR THE

GREAT NORTHERN RAILWAY.

WHEELS 4-4-2 and 6. — **GENERAL DIMENSIONS.** — **GAUGE 4 ft. 8½ in.**

CYLINDERS.

Diameter (High Pressure)	14 in.
,, (Low Pressure)	23 in.
Stroke	26 in.
Valve (High Pressure)	Piston
,, (Low Pressure)	Richardson's

BOILER.

Diameter	5 ft. 1⅝ in.
Thickness of Plates	11/16 in.
Working Pressure	200 lbs.

FIREBOX.

Material	Copper
Length	9 ft. 0 in.
Width	4 ft. 10¼ in.
Depth (front)	6 ft. 4½ in.
,, (back)	4 ft. 9 in.
Thickness of Plates (sides)	⅝ in.
,, ,, (back)	⅝ in.
,, ,, (crown)	⅝ in.
,, ,, (tube)	1 in.

TUBES (SERVE).

Number	149
Diameter (outside)	2¾ in.
Length	12 ft. 4 in.

HEATING SURFACE.

	sq. ft.
Firebox	170
Tubes	2344
Total	2514
Grate Area	31 sq. ft.

DRIVING WHEELS.

Diameter on Tread	6 ft. 8 in.
,, of Centre	6 ft. 2 in.
Journals	8½ × 9 in.

BOGIE WHEELS.

Diameter on Tread	3 ft. 2 in.
Journals	5¾ in. × 9 in.

TRAILING WHEELS.

Diameter	3 ft. 8 in.
Journals	5½ in. × 10 in.

WHEEL BASE.

Driving	8 ft. 6 in.
Rigid	15 ft. 3 in.
Total (Engine)	28 ft. 3 in.
Total (Engine and Tender)	49 ft. 6 in.

FITTINGS.

Starting Valve	Vulcan's
Reversing Gear	,,
Injectors, Combination No. 10,	Gresham & Craven's
Sight Feed Lubricators	Dewrance's
Steam Sanding	Gresham & Craven's
Carriage Warming Apparatus	

BRAKE.

Engine	Automatic Vacuum
Tender	,, ,,

WEIGHT.

On Drivers	37 tons
On Bogie	20¼ tons
On Trailing Wheels	13¾ tons
Total (Engine)	71 tons
Total (Engine and Tender)	112 tons

TENDER.

Diameter of Wheels	4 ft. 2 in.
Tank Capacity	3,670 gallons
Tender, loaded	41 tons

SERVICE.

Fast Passenger

A page from the Vulcan catalogue showing No. 1300, an experimental design for the Great Northern Railway, specifically built in 1905 to compete against the latter's prototype compound Atlantics. The design was based on the De Glehn principle with four cylinders (high pressure 14in. × 26in., low pressure 23in. × 26in.), and a boiler pressure of 200lbs.sq.in. A Vulcan patent valve admitting high pressure steam to all cylinders on starting was provided. No. 1300 survived for many years in main line duties and was finally rebuilt as a standard 2-cylinder Atlantic.

Compounding had been the vogue in England and the overseas British C.M.Es resolved to try this, one result being this large 4-cylinder 4-6-0 express passenger design for the 5ft. 6in. gauge Buenos Ayres Great Southern Railway in 1907. It was a balanced compound with h.p. cylinders 14in. × 23in. and 14in. × 26in. l.p., coupled wheels 6ft. diameter and a boiler pressure of 220lbs—regarded as high for the period.

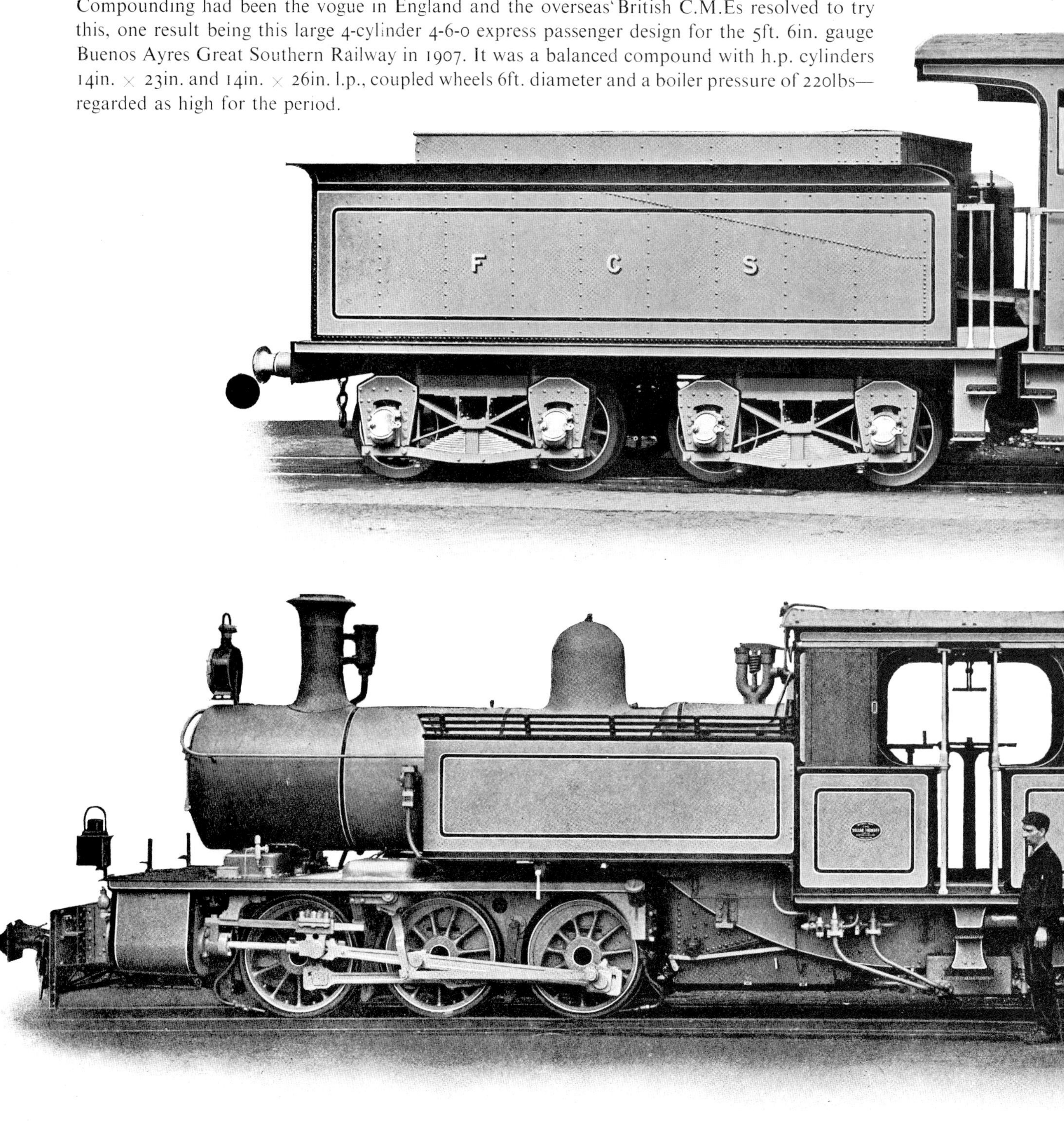

Modified Fairlie 0-6-6-0, shipped out for the Burma Railways in 1907, displayed many improvements over earlier types. Boilers were separated and a deep girder frame provided. Bogie pivots were arranged behind the bogie centres and steam reversing gear was fitted.

VULCAN LOCOMOTIVE WORKS.

STANDARD BOGIE PASSENGER ENGINE AND TENDER

FOR THE

BOMBAY BARODA AND CENTRAL INDIA RAILWAY.

WHEELS 4 - 6 - 0 and 6. GENERAL DIMENSIONS. GAUGE, 5 ft, 6 in.

CYLINDERS.	
Diameter	20in.
Stroke	26in.
Valve	Richardson's

BOILER.	
Diameter (inside)	4ft. 9⅞in.
Length	15ft. 6in.
Thickness of Plates	$\frac{9}{16}$in.
Working Pressure	180lbs.

FIRE BOX.	
Material	Copper
Length (inside at top)	7ft. 5⅜in.
Width ,, ,,	4ft. 5¼in.
Depth, Front	6ft. 5¾in.
,, Back	4ft. 9¼in.
Thickness of Plates	$\frac{9}{16}$in.
,, ,, Tube	1in.

TUBES.	
Number	201
Diameter (outside)	2¼in.
Length (between tubeplates)	15ft. 10½in.

HEATING SURFACE.	sq. ft.
Fire Box	157
Tubes	1880
Total	2037
Grate Area	32

DRIVING WHEELS.	
Diameter on Tread	6ft. 2in.
Diameter of Centre	5ft. 8in.
Journals	8in. x 9in.

BOGIE WHEELS.	
Diameter on Tread	3ft. 7in.
Journals	6¼in. x 9in.

WHEEL BASE.	
Rigid	14ft. 3in.
Total, Engine	27ft. 3in.
Total, Engine and Tender	51ft. 7in.

FITTINGS.	
Injectors	Gresham & Craven's No. 10
Sight Feed Lubricator	Detroit Bull's eye Pattern

BRAKE.	
Engine	Automatic Vacuum
Tender	Automatic Vacuum

WEIGHT.	Tons
On Drivers	49¾
On Bogie	17½
Total, Engine	67¼
Total, Engine and Tender	113¾

TENDER.	
Diameter of Wheels	3ft. 7in.
Journals	6in. x 11in.
Tank Capacity	4000 Gallons
Fuel Capacity	7½ Tons of Coal
Tender Loaded	46½ Tons

SERVICE.

Fast Passenger.

The 'H' class two-cylinder 4-6-0 for the Bombay, Baroda & Central India Railway was a forerunner of the famous 'HP' class standard locomotives for the broad gauge. These engines, constructed in 1907, were simple and of rugged construction and soon took over most of the heavy main line passenger services.

This design of standard goods engine for the North Western Railway incorporated many features commonplace in contemporary British practice, being a simple design built from 1908 onwards by the hundred for the broad gauge Indian systems. Cylinders $18\frac{1}{2}$in. × 26in., driving wheels 5ft. 1in.

This East Indian Railway 4-4-2 express passenger locomotive, built in 1908, was an unusual type for India. In service they proved adequate for lighter main line trains and survived to be rebuilt in 1938 with outside bearings to the trailing truck. Cylinders 19in. × 26in.; coupled wheels 6ft. 6in. diameter.

The 'H' class 2-8-0 heavy goods of 1909, illustrated here, was the forerunner of the 'HGS' classes, which became a standard Indian broad gauge type. Cylinders 21in. × 26in.; driving wheels 4ft. $8\frac{1}{2}$in.; total weight 118 tons; tender coal capacity $7\frac{1}{2}$ tons.

The 'HG' class 2-8-0s were the standard heavy goods locomotives produced in 1910 onwards for the Indian broad gauge lines. Dimensions were similar to 'H' class, but the drive was moved to the third axle and the cylinder layout improved.

4-4-0 fast passenger type for the Madras & Southern Mahratta Railway, 1910; simple and sturdy, these machines were the second string in the passenger types; cylinders 18½in. × 26in.; driving wheels 6 ft. 2in.

By 1910 the larger metre gauge railways of India required more powerful passenger locomotives to cope with increased traffic and that year these well-proportioned 4-6-0s were built. Simple, robust machines, they were produced in various batches, this example being No. 142 for the Eastern Bengal Railway. Cylinders 15½in. × 22in.; coupled wheels 4ft.9in.

The large 0-6-6-0 Fairlies, built for the Mexican Railways in 1911, weighed 138 tons. They could haul 300 tons over gradients of 1 in 25 and traverse curves of 330ft. radius. Cylinders 19in. × 25in.; driving wheels 4ft. diameter.

4-4-0 No. 1291 on the Great Indian Peninsula Railway was a repeat of an earlier design for the broad gauge, ordered for lighter main line services. By the year 1911, most Indian railways were concentrating on six- and eight-coupled types. Cylinders $18\frac{1}{2}$in. × 26in.; driving wheels 6ft. 6in.

No. 25

VULCAN LOCOMOTIVE WORKS.

STANDARD TANK ENGINE FOR THE EAST INDIAN RAILWAY.

WHEELS 2-6-4.	GENERAL DIMENSIONS	GAUGE, 5 ft.

CYLINDERS.

Diameter	18 in.
Stroke	26 in.

BOILER.

Diameter (inside)	5 ft. 0 in.
Length	11 ft. 0 in.
Thickness of Plates	9/16 in.
Working Pressure	180 lbs.

FIREBOX.

Material	Copper
Length (inside, at top)	6 ft. 5⅜ in.
Width " "	4 ft. 3⅝ in.
Depth (front)	6 ft. 5¾ in.
" (back)	5 ft. 6¼ in.
Thickness of Plates	9/16 in.
" " Tube Plate	1 in.

TUBES.

Number	210
Diameter (outside)	2 in.
Length (between tube plates)	11 ft. 4½ in.

HEATING SURFACE.

	Sq. ft.
Fire Box	150
Tubes	1250
Total	1400
Grate Area	27 sq. ft.

DRIVING WHEELS.

Diameter on Tread	5 ft. 1½ in.
" of Centre	4 ft. 7½ in.
Journals	8 in. by 9 in.

BOGIE WHEELS.

Diameter on Tread	3 ft. 7 in.
Journals	6¼ in. by 9 in.

WHEEL BASE.

Rigid	13 ft. 0 in.
Total	34 ft. 3 in.

FITTINGS.

Injectors	Gresham & Craven's
Sight Feed Lubricators	Hulburd's
Steam Sanding	Gresham & Craven's
Metallic Packing	United Kingdom
Reversing Gear	Steam and Hand

BRAKE.

Hand.

Vacuum brake for working train.

Tank capacity	2,000
Fuel Capacity	3 tons

WEIGHT.

On Radial Bogie	9
On Drivers	4
On Hind Bogie	2
Total	7

SERVICE.

Passenger.

In 1912 there was an urgent need for suburban passenger engines to deal with the rapidly increasing traffic in India and a batch of these modern tank locomotives were delivered. With 2-6-4 type wheel arrangement, they were closely patterned on their British contemporaries. Cylinders 18in. × 26in., driving wheels 5ft. 2in.

No. 28

VULCAN LOCOMOTIVE WORKS.

BOGIE TANK ENGINE FOR THE CENTRAL URUGUAY RAILWAY.

HEELS 4-4-4.	GENERAL DIMENSIONS	GAUGE, 4 ft. $8\frac{1}{2}$ in.

CYLINDERS.

eter	16 in.
e	24 in.

BOILER.

eter (inside)	4 ft. 1 in.
h	10 ft. 1 in.
ness of Plates	$\frac{1}{2}$ in.
ing Pressure	160 lbs.

FIREBOX

ial	Copper.
h (inside, at top)	4 ft. $10\frac{1}{2}$ in.
1 " "	3 ft. $7\frac{3}{4}$ in.
1 (front)	5 ft. 3 in.
(back)	4 ft. $4\frac{1}{2}$ in.
ness of Plates	$\frac{1}{2}$ in.
" " Tube Plate	$\frac{15}{16}$ in.

TUBES.

Number	171
Diameter (outside)	$1\frac{7}{8}$ in.
Length (between tube plates)	10 ft. $4\frac{5}{16}$ in.

HEATING SURFACE.

	Sq. ft.
Fire Box	94.1
Tubes	869.0
Total	963.1

Grate Area	17.5 sq. ft.

DRIVING WHEELS.

Diameter on Tread	5 ft. 0 in.
" of Centre	4 ft. 6 in.
Journals	$7\frac{1}{2}$ in. by 9 in.

BOGIE WHEELS.

Diameter on Tread	2 ft. $9\frac{1}{2}$ in.
Journals	$5\frac{1}{4}$ in. by 9 in.

WHEEL BASE.

Rigid	7 ft. 0 in.
Total	29 ft. $8\frac{1}{2}$ in.

FITTINGS.

Injectors	Gresham & Craven's No. 8
Sight Feed Lubricators	Wakefield's
Sanding	Hand
Metallic Packing	United Kingdom
Reversing Gear	Hand
Draw Springs	Spencer Moulton

BRAKE.

Hand.
Vacuum.

Tank Capacity	1,650 gallons
Fuel Capacity	3 tons of Coal

WEIGHT.

On Drivers	30 tons
On Bogie (front)	$14\frac{3}{4}$ tons
On Bogie (hind)	16 tons
Total	$60\frac{3}{4}$ tons

SERVICE.

Passenger.

An unusual locomotive turned out in 1915 for the standard gauge Central Uruguay Railway was 4-4-4T No. 41. An axle load of fifteen tons permitted wide use on lightly laid track, allied to severe curvature. The engines were well liked and simple to maintain. Cylinders 16in. × 24in.; driving wheels 5ft. diameter.

WHEELS 2-8-0 and 8. GOODS ENGINE AND TENDER. FRENCH ARTILLERY DEPARTMENT. GAUGE, 1440 m/m

CYLINDERS.

Diameter .... 590 m/m
Stroke .... 650 m/m
Valve .... Piston

BOILER.

Diameter (inside) .... 1714 m/m
Length .... 4350 m/m
Thickness of Plates .... 17 m/m
Working Pressure .... 12 kilos per sq. c/m

FIREBOX.

Material .... Copper
Length (inside at top) .... 2684 m/m
Width ,, ,, ... 1375 m/m
Depth (front) .... 2208 m/m
,, (back) .... 1608 m/m
Thickness of Plates .... 16 m/m
,, ,, (Tube) .... 28 m/m

TUBES.

Number .... small 174, large 24
Diameter (outside) .... small 50 m/m, large 133 m/m
Length (between tube plates) .... 4500 m/m

HEATING SURFACE.

	sq. metres.
Fire Box	16·9
Tubes (small)	110·69
,, (large)	42·41
Total	170·00
Superheater	36·60
Total	206·60
Grate Area	3·16

DRIVING WHEELS.

Diameter on Tread .... 1440 m/m
,, of Centre .... 1300 m/m
Journals .... 210 × 250 m/m

PONY TRUCK WHEELS.

Diameter on Tread .... 850 m/m
Journals .... 145 × 260 m/m

WHEEL BASE.

Rigid .... 5100 m/m
Total (Engine) .... 7600 m/m
Total (Engine and Tender) .... 16350 m/m

FITTINGS.

Injectors .... Gresham & Craven's No. 10 Friedmann
Sight Feed Lubricator .... Detroit 5 Feed
Metallic Packing .... United States
Speed Indicator .... Flaman
Sanding .... Leach Pneumatic

BRAKE.

Engine .... Westinghouse High Pressure
Tender .... ,, ,, ,,

WEIGHT.

On Drivers .... 65 tons
On Pony Truck .... $8\frac{3}{4}$ tons
Total (Engine) .... $73\frac{3}{4}$ tons
Total (Engine and Tender) .... 118 tons

TENDER.

Diameter of Wheels .... 960 m/m
Journals .... 130 m/m × 240 m/m
Tank Capacity .... 3960 gallons
Fuel Capacity .... $4\frac{3}{4}$ tons of coal
Tender, loaded .... $44\frac{1}{4}$ tons

SERVICE.

Goods.

Postal Address: NEWTON-LE-WILLOWS, LANCASHIRE.

T. H. SMITH, PRINTER, EARLESTOWN.

By 1917 the demands of the Great War had ravaged the motive power on French railways and in that year the French Artillery Department ordered a batch of powerful 2-8-0 tender locomotives to an existing French design for freight traffic. Cylinders 22in. × 26in., driving wheels 4ft. 9in. diameter.

Finalisation of the 'HP' type 4-6-0 appeared in 1921 and this particular engine, one of a batch delivered to the Great Indian Peninsula Railway for fast passenger service, was No. 411, the War Memorial engine *Hero*. So successful were these engines that a large batch, updated in design, were built as late as 1946. Cylinders $20\frac{1}{2}$in. × 26in., driving wheels 6ft. 2in. diameter.

A photograph of 4-cylinder 4-6-0 mixed-traffic locomotive No. 464, turned out in 1921 for the Great Central Railway shortly before the grouping. These massive machines were more successful than their passenger counterparts. Heavy on coal, but powerful, their small grate area did not tell on them so severely due to their relatively slow speed duties. Cylinders 16in. × 26in., coupled wheels 5ft. 7in.

A large order for Midland type 0-6-0 tank locomotives, adopted as an LMS standard design, was turned out from Vulcan Foundry in 1922. These long-lived machines were to be seen on all parts of the system and several have been preserved. Cylinders 18in. × 26in., driving wheels 4ft. 7in.

With their extensive network of lightly laid track, the 5ft. 6in. gauge Ceylon Government Railways sponsored various rather unusual designs including this 4-6-0, built in 1922. The distribution of the water supply was intended to help spread the load and the tender is unique, with one bogie and one pair of fixed wheels.

The famous long-boilered Vulcan 4-8-2 goods were built in 1924 for the 3ft. 6in. gauge Gold Coast Railway. Simple and robust, with ample boiler capacity, these heavy freight locomotives are understood to be still in use on sections of the Ghana Railways. Cylinders $19\frac{1}{2}$in. × 24in., driving wheels 3ft. 9in. With minor improvements this design was turned out in batches for over thirty years.

A batch of modern 2-6-4 tank locomotives as built in 1925 for the Buenos Ayres Great Southern, including No. 3584. These proved to be very successful in suburban service and lasted until the advent of diesel-electric locomotives, again Vulcan-built, in 1958.

Produced in 1926 for express passenger service on the Buenos Ayres Great Southern Railway was this oil-fired 3-cylinder 4-6-2 built in 1926. The diminutive trailing truck was reluctantly incorporated to reduce the axle loading and rendered this class of locomotives slightly less sure-footed on starting than they would have been as 4-6-0s. Cylinders 19in. × 26in.; coupled wheels 6ft. 6in. diameter.

r example of the long-boilered 4-8-2 goods photographed outside the works in 1949, undergoing steaming trials prior to shipment to Ghana.

An era of new standard locomotives for India for both broad and metre gauge was heralded in 1927 by the construction of the 'YD' class 2-8-2 for the metre gauge. This versatile mixed-traffic machine was soon in great demand by C.M.Es on various of the Indian railways and was turned out in batches over many years. Cylinders were 16in. × 24in., driving wheels 4ft. Total weight, engine and tender, was 80 tons and tractive effort (at 90 per cent) 20,737lbs.

Two designs that show the diverse range of main line locomotive types being produced by
Foundry in the 1920s. Above is No. 801, a massive 3-cylinder 2-8-2 built for Nigerian Railways i
Noteworthy machines both for their size for 3ft. 6in. gauge and for the use of three cylinders, the
named for Government officials. Cylinders 18in. × 28in., driving wheels 4ft. 6in.; total weight

·low, No. 1184, an example of the large batch of modified Midland compounds constructed for SR in 1925. Although modest in dimension, these 4-4-0s did some impressive work before being ded by the 'Royal Scots'. Cylinder dimensions (3)—H.P. 19in. × 26in., L.P. 21in. × 26in.; wheels 6ft. 9in.

For the broad gauge Indian State Railways, the 'maid of all work' 'XD' class was introduced—a large 2-8-2 with generous boiler and 17-ton axleload. These found immediate favour in service and were probably the most successful of the 'X' types, being built in batches over a period of 20 years. Cylinders $22\frac{1}{2}$in. × 28in.; driving wheels 5ft. 1in. diameter.

Indian express passenger needs were catered for by the 'XB' class of Pacific type. The bold dimensions of these engines were not fully matched by the front end design and their riding at speed was dramatically improved after the serious Bihta accident in 1931. Elimination of the Cartazzi slides on the trailing truck and improved bogie side control restored the locomotives to normal speed restrictions. Cylinders $21\frac{1}{2}$in. × 28in.; coupled wheels 6ft. 2in.

Built in 1928, the largest and most powerful Indian express passenger locomotive was of the 'XC' type, only restricted in numbers by the 20-ton axleloading. Cylinders 23in. × 28in.; coupled wheels 6ft. 2in.

The heaviest of the new 'X' types, the 'XE' class was the most powerful freight locomotive in the Indian sub-continent. A great advance on the existing 2-8-0 types, these locomotives were unrivalled in slow speed slogging with 1,500 ton loads, and repeat orders were still being delivered up to 1947. The mediocre front end design did not hamper these locomotives due to their slower speed. Cylinders $23\frac{1}{2}$in. × 30in.; driving wheels 5ft. 1in. diameter.

The lightest of the broad gauge standard types, the 'XA' Pacific was an elaborate miniature of the 'XB' and 'XC' types. An axleloading of 13 tons permitted wide route availability on the Indian Railways and a large number were constructed from 1929 onwards.

To complete the metre gauge standard locomotives for India came the 'YC', heaviest of the 'Y' series for passenger work. A typically neat machine and successful in service, they were built in quantity over a number of years.

Metre gauge 'YB' class passenger locomotives were turned out in 1928. They were an instant success and C.M.Es were budgeting annually for more. The design was adopted in Burma as well as India as their light axleload permitted widespread use. Cylinders 16in. × 24in.; coupled wheels 4ft. 9in.

ur experimental
cifics were turned
t in 1930 classed as
S1' and 'XS2'.
ese were virtually
odified 'XC' Pacifics,
ng fitted with
protti & Lentz
ve gear
pectively.
aintenance with
se valve gears was
roblem and the
lian experience
ralleled that of
lways in Britain.

Vulcan Foundry also constructed electric locomotives for India, the first of these for main line freight use being built in conjunction with Metropolitan Vickers in 1929 for the broad gauge Great Indian Peninsula Railway. These 123-ton machines, using 1,500 volts D.C. overhead supply, were used for banking up the Ghat inclines and had a rated capacity of 2,600 h.p.

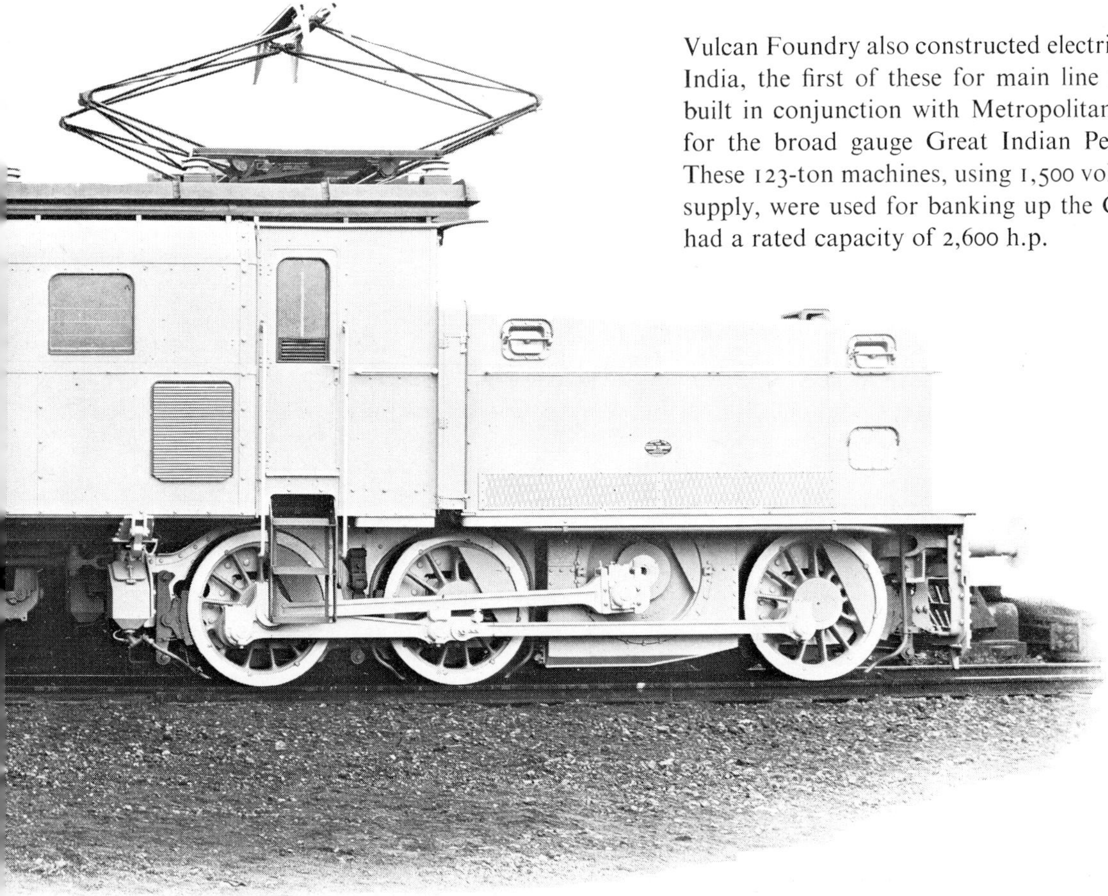

THE VULCAN LOCOMOTIVE WORKS.

GOODS ENGINE AND TENDER

FOR THE

NIGERIAN RAILWAY.

FITTED WITH SUPERHEATER
(MULTIPLE VALVE HEADER).

WHEELS, 4-8-2 & 8. GENERAL DIMENSIONS. GAUGE 3 ft. 6 ins.

CYLINDERS (3)

Diameter	18¾ in.
Stroke	24 in.
Valve	Piston

BOILER.

Diameter (inside)	5 ft. 9⅛ in.
Length (Total)	29 ft. 6 in.
Thickness of Plates	$\frac{11}{16}$ & $\frac{1}{32}$ in.
Working Pressure	200 lb.

FIREBOX (With combustion chamber).

Material	Steel
Length (inside at top)	10 ft. 5½ in.
Width (,, ,,)	5 ft. 3¼ in.
Depth (front)	6 ft. 4 in.
,, (back)	5 ft. 4½ in.
Thickness of Plates	⅜ in.
,, ,, Tube	$\frac{9}{16}$ in.

TUBES.

136 Tubes (diameter outside)	2¼ in.
30 Smoke Tubes (diameter outside)	5½ in.
4 Arch Tubes (diameter outside)	3 in.
Length (between tube plates)	18 ft. 0 in.

HEATING SURFACE.

Fire Box	218 sq. ft.
Tubes	2,235 sq. ft.
Total	2,453 sq. ft.
Superheater	607 sq. ft.
Grate Area	45 sq. ft.

DRIVING WHEELS.

Diameter on Tread	4 ft. 6 in.
Do. of Centre	4 ft. 0½in.
Journals	8¼ in. × 10 in.

LEADING BOGIE WHEELS.

Diameter on Tread	2 ft. 9 in.
Journals	5½ in. × 8½ in.

HIND TRUCK.

Diameter on Tread	2 ft. 9 in.
Journals	6 in. × 12⅛ in.

WHEEL BASE.

Rigid	14 ft. 9 in.
Total (Engine)	34 ft. 2 in.
Total (Engine and Tender)	61 ft. 0½ in.

FITTINGS.

Injectors (2)	Gresham & Craven's No. 9
Feed Pump	Weir's
Sight Feed Lubricator (2) 4 feeds	Detroit

BRAKE.

Engine	Steam
Tender	Hand

Vacuum Brake for working Train.

WEIGHT.

On Drivers	66 tons
On Truck (Front)	13½ tons
On Truck (Hind)	10¾ tons
Total (Engine)	90¼ tons
Total (Engine and Tender)	138¾ tons
Tractive Effort at 90 per cent.	42,186 lbs.
Ratio of Adhesion at 90 per cent.	3·5

TENDER.

Diameter of Wheels	2 ft. 9 in.
Journals	5 in. × 10 in.
Tank Capacity	4,500 gallons
Fuel Capacity	8 tons
Tender, loaded	48½ tons

SERVICE.

Goods.

The Nigerian Railways received these massive 3-cylinder freight locomotives in 1930. An enlargement of the 1925 design, they were an outstanding advance for the 3ft. 6in. gauge and were probably the most modern design operating in the African continent at that period.

THE VULCAN LOCOMOTIVE WORKS.

MIXED TRAFFIC ENGINE AND TENDER.

FOR THE

LONDON MIDLAND AND SCOTTISH RAILWAY.

(FITTED WITH SUPERHEATER)

Vulcan were awarded a large contract for these outstanding mixed traffic 4-6-0s to the design of W. A. Stanier, then newly appointed Chief Mechanical Engineer to the LMSR. These engines were delivered simultaneously with the initial batch of locomotives being built at Crewe in 1934. A repeat order was received in 1936 with increased superheater arrangements.

Stanier Class 5 No. 5030 awaiting departure from Vulcan Foundry for delivery to Crewe in 1936.

WEIGHT IN
WORKING ORDER.................$34\frac{1}{4}$ tons...$33\frac{1}{2}$ tons.......................................$10\frac{3}{4}$ tons......................18 tons

TOTAL WEIGHT, TENDER......$67\frac{3}{4}$ TONS.

TRACTIVE EFFORT AT 90% BOILER PRESSURE = 28,425 LBS.

WHEELS 4-6-2 & 4-4.

GENERAL DIMENSIC

CYLINDERS.

Diameter..19 in.
Stroke...28 in.
Piston Valve...............................Diameter 10 in.

BOILER.

Diameter (inside) ....5 ft. 6 in.
Length (between tube plates)...............14 ft. 0 in.
Thickness of Plates...... ....$\frac{3}{4}$ in.
Working Pressure.................................225 lbs.

FIREBOX.

Material...Steel
Length (inside at top).... ....9 ft. $6\frac{3}{8}$ in.
Depth (front) .... 6 ft. $1\frac{3}{8}$ in.
,, (back) ....5 ft. $4\frac{7}{8}$ in.
Thickness of Plates.......................... ....$\frac{3}{8}$ in.
,, ,, Tube...........................$\frac{1}{2}$ in.

TUBES.

115 Tubes (diameter outside).......................$2\frac{1}{8}$ in.
34 Smoke Tubes (diameter outside) ... .$5\frac{1}{4}$ in.
Length (between tube plates)..............14 ft. 0 in.

HEATING SURFACE.

Sq. ft.
Fire Box.......................... 190
Tubes..1550

Total.........1740

Sq. ft.
Superheater..428
Grate Area...32.6

DRIVING WHEELS.

Diameter on Tread................ ....6 ft. 0 in.
,, of Centre. ....5 ft. 6 in.
Journals...9 in. × 10 in.

BOGIE.

Diameter on Tread....... ....3 ft. 2 in.
Journals.......................................$6\frac{1}{2}$ in. × 11 in.

Diameter
Journals .

Rigid......
Total (En
Total (En

1 Injecto
1 ,,

Sight Fe
Electric

Engine ..
Tender...
Vacuum

Modern locomotives were now required for South America and for the Buenos Ayres Great Southern Railway two handsome designs were produced. In 1938 the '12K' class Pacific appeared for fast passenger work. Neat in design, these engines had many parts interchangeable with the '15A' class seen overleaf. Cylinders 19in. × 28in.; coupled wheels 6ft. 0in.

s........................18 tons....................................23¾ tons.

NE......88½ TONS. TOTAL WEIGHT ENGINE AND TENDER 156¼ TONS.

VE EFFORT TO ADHESION AT 90% = 4·26.

GAUGE, 5 ft. 6 in.

ₓ.

............4 ft. 0½ in.

......6½ in. × 11 in.

E.

............14 ft. 0 in.

.... 33 ft. 1 in.

.........60 ft. 10¾ in.

& Craven's No. 10

alfe Exhaust Steam Class "H"

............Wakefield.

................Stone's.

...............Vacuum.

Vacuum and Hand.

n.

WEIGHT.

On Drivers	54 tons.
On Bogie	23¾ tons.
On Hind Truck	10¾ tons.
Total (Engine)	88½ tons.
Total (Engine and Tender)	156¼ tons.
Tractive Effort @ 90%	28,425 lbs.
Ratio of Adhesion @ 90%	4.26.

TENDER.

Diameter of Wheels	3 ft. 2 in.
Journals	6½ in. × 11 in.
Tank Capacity	6000 gallons.
Fuel Capacity	11 tons Oil.
Tender, loaded	67¾ tons.

SERVICE.

Passenger.

Noteworthy for their dimensions and the delivery problems that came later, were these giant 4-8-4 tender locomotives. The Boxer Indemnity Fund permitted the Chinese National Railways in 1936 to order 24 of these giant machines, which turned the scale at 192 tons. These engines were equipped with mechanical stokers and grease-lubricated throughout. Delivery coincided with the Sino-Japanese war and miracles were achieved in preventing these engines falling into the hands of the invaders. Successful in traffic, survivors of the class have been identified in service as late as 1966. Cylinders $20\frac{7}{8}$in. × $29\frac{1}{2}$in.; driving wheels 5ft. 8in.

A highly successful mixed traffic type '15A' class 4-8-0 used the same boiler and cylinders as the '12K' class. They became a standard fast freight and passenger engine for the system and a large repeat batch was delivered after World War II. Driving wheels 5ft. 8in.

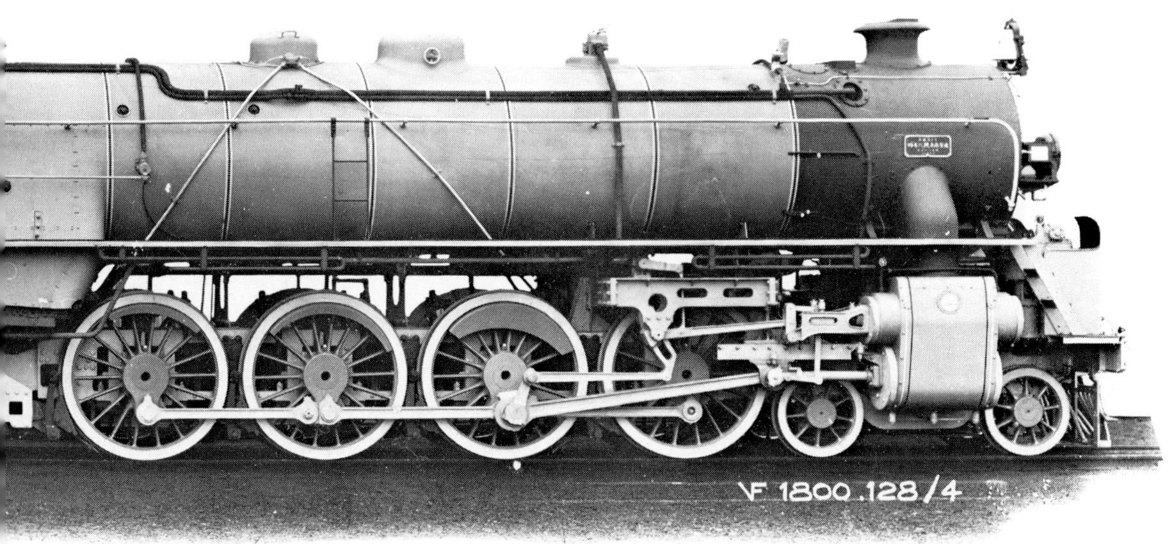

Another view of one of the 4-8-4s delivered to China, photographed outside the Works prior to despatch.

No. **67A**

THE VULCAN LOCOMOTIVE WORKS.

GOODS ENGINE AND TENDER

FOR THE

GOLD COAST RAILWAY.

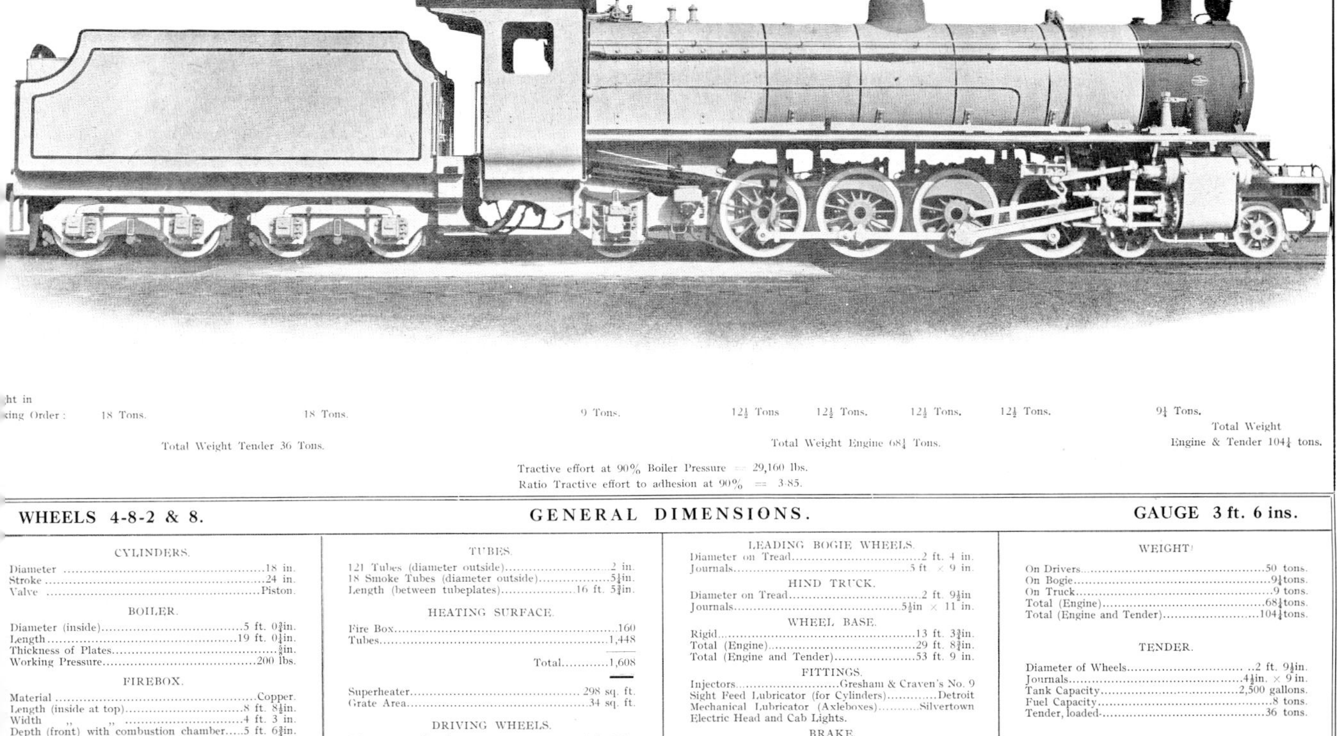

ht in
king Order: 18 Tons. 18 Tons. 9 Tons. 12½ Tons 12½ Tons. 12½ Tons. 12½ Tons. 9¼ Tons.

Total Weight Tender 36 Tons. Total Weight Engine 68¼ Tons. Total Weight Engine & Tender 104¼ tons.

Tractive effort at 90% Boiler Pressure = 29,160 lbs.
Ratio Tractive effort to adhesion at 90% = 3·85.

WHEELS 4-8-2 & 8. **GENERAL DIMENSIONS.** **GAUGE 3 ft. 6 ins.**

CYLINDERS.

Diameter .... 18 in.
Stroke .... 24 in.
Valve .... Piston.

BOILER.

Diameter (inside) .... 5 ft. 0¾in.
Length .... 19 ft. 0¼in.
Thickness of Plates .... ⅝in.
Working Pressure .... 200 lbs.

FIREBOX.

Material .... Copper.
Length (inside at top) .... 8 ft. 8½in.
Width ,, ,, ... 4 ft. 3 in.
Depth (front) with combustion chamber .... 5 ft. 6¾in.
,, (back) .... 4 ft. 6 in.
Thickness of Plates .... 9/16 in.
,, ,, Tube .... 1 in.

TUBES.

121 Tubes (diameter outside) .... 2 in.
18 Smoke Tubes (diameter outside) .... 5¼in.
Length (between tubeplates) .... 16 ft. 5¾in.

HEATING SURFACE.

Fire Box 160
Tubes 1,448
Total 1,608

Superheater .... 298 sq. ft.
Grate Area .... 34 sq. ft.

DRIVING WHEELS.

Diameter on Tread .... 4 ft. 0 in.
,, of Centre .... 3 ft. 6 in.
Journals .... 7½in. × 8 in.

LEADING BOGIE WHEELS.

Diameter on Tread .... 2 ft. 4 in.
Journals .... 5 ft × 9 in.

HIND TRUCK.

Diameter on Tread .... 2 ft. 9½in
Journals .... 5½in × 11 in.

WHEEL BASE.

Rigid .... 13 ft. 3¾in.
Total (Engine) .... 29 ft. 8¾in.
Total (Engine and Tender) .... 53 ft. 9 in.

FITTINGS.

Injectors .... Gresham & Craven's No. 9
Sight Feed Lubricator (for Cylinders) .... Detroit
Mechanical Lubricator (Axleboxes) .... Silvertown
Electric Head and Cab Lights.

BRAKE.

Engine .... Steam
Tender .... Vacuum & Hand
Vacuum Brake for working Train.

WEIGHT.

On Drivers .... 50 tons.
On Bogie .... 9¼tons.
On Truck .... 9 tons.
Total (Engine) .... 68¼tons.
Total (Engine and Tender) .... 104¼tons.

TENDER.

Diameter of Wheels .... 2 ft. 9½in.
Journals .... 4½in. × 9 in.
Tank Capacity .... 2,500 gallons.
Fuel Capacity .... 8 tons.
Tender, loaded .... 36 tons.

SERVICE.

Goods.

Postal Address: NEWTON-LE-WILLOWS, LANCS., ENGLAND.

McCorquodale & Co., Ltd., Printers, Newton-le-Willows.

For the Gold Coast Railway a further batch of modified Vulcan long goods 4-8-2 tender locomotives was built in 1939, redesigned with bar frames and many detail improvements. A number were shipped immediately prior to World War II.

evelopment of roller bearings for railway application had now ached a successful stage and, in line with the cautious approach of ilways in Britain, India decided to order two experimental Pacifics r the broad gauge; the result was the 'XP' class, midway in mensions between 'XB' and 'XC' types, fitted with Timken and K.F. bearings respectively. All carrying axles were equipped. rformance was generally good.

Modernisation of the broad gauge Indian suburban traffic was urgent and a series of new 2-6-4 and 2-6-2 tank locomotives were built in 1939 and delivered in naval convoy during 1940. These two types were identical machines apart from increased coal and water in the 2-6-4 machines. Noteworthy at this period was the lightweight all-welded superstructure. The type became a 'W' standard and a large repeat batch was delivered in 1951.

Unusual for the period (1940) were a number of light passenger 2-4-2 tank locomotives for the East Indian Railway; however, the order was not repeated.

standard shunting tank for the larger yards in India s turned out in 1940. This incorporated the same light-ight all-welded superstructure as the 'WM' locomotives.

World War II brought a virtual cessation of normal locomotive building for export and instead w
production was commenced, notably of the 'Matilda' tank. Several years of intensive production
machine took place, but in 1943 the Government ordered all-out effort to produce the 2-8-0 'Au

tives. Based on the Stanier 8F 2-8-0, but with simplified boiler and built from austerity materials, o of these powerful machines were produced between 1943 and 1945. These scenes were taken in 943.

Cessation of hostilities left Europe's railways devastated and an international design was quickly worked out at Vulcan, resulting in the 'Liberation' 2-8-0, a massive machine sponsored by United Nations Relief Organisation. 110 of these were delivered to Poland, Yugoslavia, Czechoslovakia and Luxembourg. Cylinders $21\frac{5}{8}$in. × 28in.; coupled wheels 4ft. 9in.

To meet the urgent needs of the war-strained railways of India, a large contract for the well tried 'HP/S' design of locomotive was turned out in 1946/47. A completely modernised version was evolved and seventy locomotives were shipped in all.

Nigeria was the venue of the abortive Ground-nuts Scheme and in 1948, to assist in hauling the expected crops, a batch of neat 2-8-2s, the famous 'River' class, was produced for the Nigerian Railways. These were an instant success and many more were constructed.

At home, the LNER, after the long regime of Sir Nigel Gresley, turned to two-cylinder locomotives and fifty Class 'B.1' 4-6-0 mixed traffic machines were produced, finished in lined apple-green livery, heralding a new standard type. Cylinders 20in. × 26in.; coupled wheels 6ft. 2in.

In 1939 the Turkish State Railways had placed a contract with the Foundry for 22 large 2-10-0s to a German design. However, Government wartime policy prevented any construction of these until 1948. Virtually, these locomotives were a replica of a standard pre-war Reichsbahn type, with 25in. × 26in. cylinders and 4ft. 9in. coupled wheels.

56094

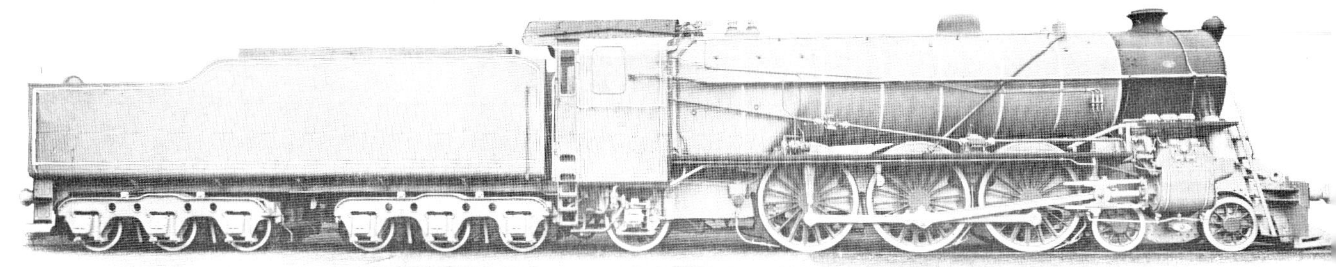

The class 'P.S.11' Pacifics built for the Central Argentine Railways were, on a power-for-weight basis, one of the most powerful passenger locomotives ever constructed. Fitted with three cylinders and Caprotti valve gear the engines, a re-design of a 1930 locomotive, earned a high reputation working 750-ton trains between Buenos Ayres and Mar del Plata. They were oil-fired and had twelve-wheeled tenders.

The Tasmanian Railways, with their light track, decided to modernise their vintage locomotive stock in 1950 and this 4-8-2 type with 12-ton axleload and S.K.F. roller bearings throughout was the result. In service the engines earned an enviable reputation and one has been preserved.

The Queensland Railways in Australia, also recovering from wartime shortages, decided to augment their well-tried BB18¼ Class Pacifics. The railway had a light track and the design was thoroughly modernised, with roller bearings throughout. They gave good service before the diesel takeover; one has been preserved.

A post-war design, the 'WG' Class 2-8-2 became a new standard for use on the Indian Government Railways. Later batches in the class were built at Chitteranjan Indian Locomotive works and in all over 1,000 of these machines were constructed.

Egypt had admired the performance of LMS type 2-8-0 WD locomotives on their tracks during World War II and a contract for similar locomotives was placed by the Egyptian State Railways in 1952. A simplified parallel boiler was fitted in place of the Stanier taper type, and other modifications were carried out; the tractive effort was similar to the LMS version.

East Africa required additional power for the metre gauge EAR system and a batch of these 2-8-2s was produced in 1952; they were compact, well equipped machines weighing 101 tons in all and with a t.e. of 26,540lbs.

The Victoria Railways in Australia, like most overseas systems, suffered from a total inability to acquire locomotives during wartime and after, and not until 1954 were sixty 2-8-0s delivered, updated from an earlier design, Class 'K'. Half of these were fitted for coal burning, the remaining thirty for oil. Cylinders 20in. × 26in.; driving wheels 4ft. 8in.

The final steam locomotive order before complete change-over to diesel and electric locomotive construction at Vulcan Foundry came in 1956. In view of this change, an Austerity version of an Indian 'Y' class locomotive, minus one coupled axle, was quickly designed to meet an order from North Borneo Railways—the result, a neat 2-6-2 tender locomotive which performed well. Cylinders 15½in. × 24in.; coupled wheels 4ft.

The Antofagasta & Bolivia Railway possesses a fearsome main line crossing the Andes and operating at high altitudes. To cope with increasing traffic over this route, a batch of handsome 4-8-2s was produced, incorporating a particularly massive boiler to cope with the heavy steam demand on constant grades. Cylinders 19in. × 26in.; coupled wheels 4ft.

Extensive wartime traffic had seriously ravaged the Persian railw
in spite of the extensive use of 'WD' locomotives and a large contr
for the most advanced freight locomotives was carried out in 19
Inevitably these machines were oil burners, and were of the 'Santa
type, *viz.* 2-10-2. The Abadan oil crisis prevented shipment for th
years and special sidings were laid in at Vulcan to accommodate the
locomotives. During this time, as a point of interest, they requir
moving monthly in view of their roller bearings.

341

East African Railways placed a large contract in 1955 for general purpose locomotives similar to the Nigerian 'River' class, but of 2-8-4 type in view of restricted axleload of 11.5 tons. These engines were oil-fired and intended to operate in Kenya and Uganda. Cylinders 17in. × 26in.; coupled wheels 4ft. This large contract was the final steam requirement for East African Railways, who then turned to diesel traction.

The first of a new lightweight Pacific design, on 'Acceptance steaming' in 1955. The relatively light axleload of 16.9 tons permitted widespread use over the broad gauge lines in India and the type was multiplied in workshops there, in many cases from parts supplied by Vulcan Works. Standing beside No. 7787 with the author and his Chief Assistant, are the Designer and the Commissioner for the Indian State Railways, together with his Inspecting Officer.

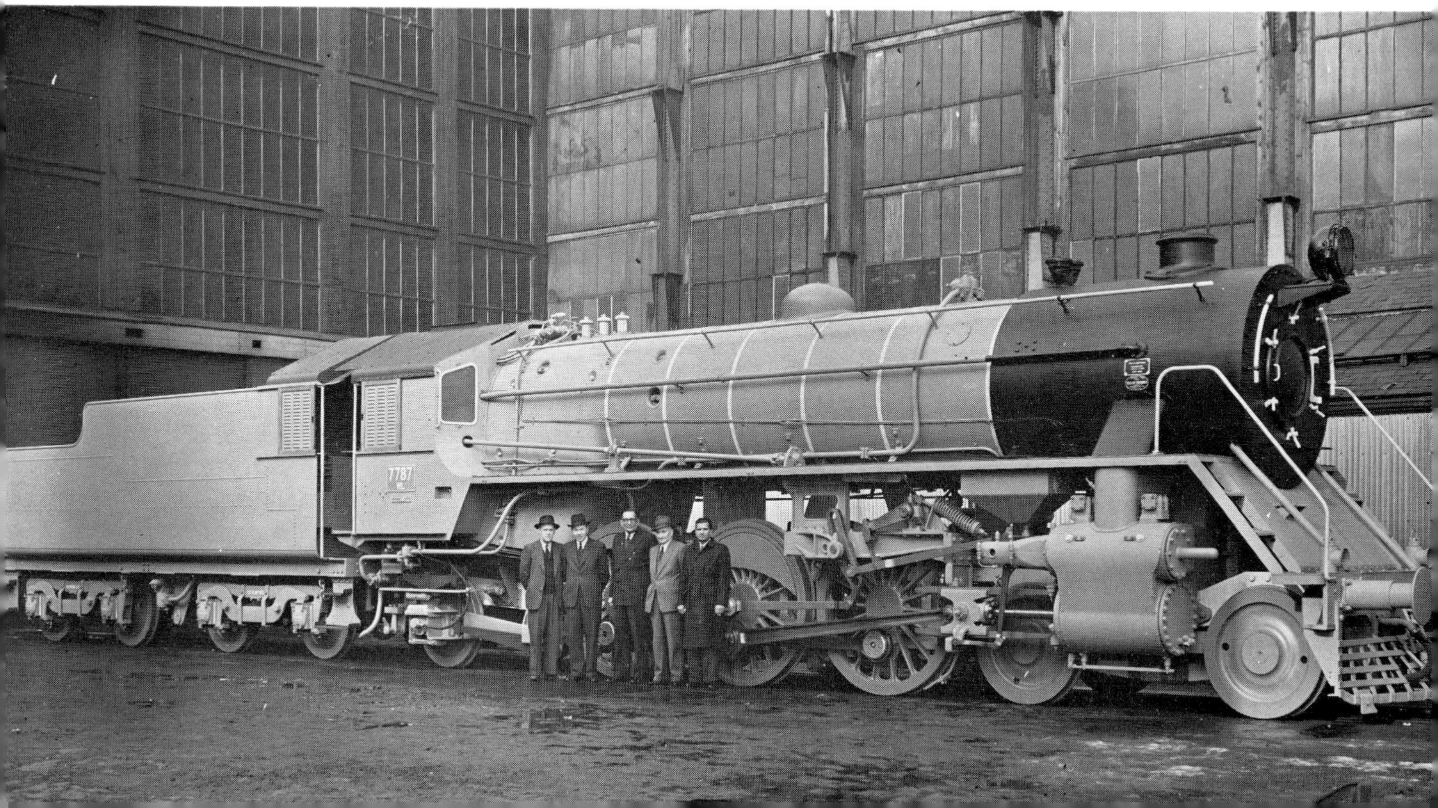

The last official steam passenger train in the North-West was run on Sunday, 11 August 1968, from Liverpool to Manchester. Appropriately enough, this was hauled by Vulcan-built Class 5 No. 45110, turned out in 1934. The train is seen here at Earlestown Junction.

The last steam shunting locomotive in the works was this four-coupled *Vulcan*, built in 1902 and seen here in retirement on the Works sports field in 1968. Still a sound steamer, it is now preserved at Lytham Industrial Museum.

Transport of large out-of-gauge locomotives to Liverpool and Birkenhead docks for shipment abroad presented great problems. Limitations of lifting capacity made it necessary for the locomotive to be broken down to suitable weights, in itself a costly procedure. However, in the 1920s, the LMSR built two special twelve-wheel bogie wagons, and for many years complete locomotives, minus the chimney and boiler mountings, were despatched by rail to the dock-side. In the early 1930s, in collaboration with a road haulage company, a special vehicle incorporating large hydraulic jacks capable of lowering and lifting the carrying platform was designed and, with the advance in ships' lifting gear capacity, plus use of a 'Mammoth' floating crane at the docks, no stripping-off of parts was involved and the complete locomotive could be despatched overseas ready for steaming. Seen here in the 1880s are a batch of Indian locomotives, broken-down ready for shipment aboard a sailing vessel.

The road transporter as used in the 1930s. Hydraulic jacks permitted lowering the platform to within an inch of the road surface and slewing was possible from the rear cabin, necessary as locomotives *en route* by road from Vulcan had a low bridge to negotiate before reaching the East Lancashire highway which led to the docks. The locomotive here is an 'HPS' class for Indian Government Railways, photographed on its way to Liverpool.

Inset: One of the two special bogie wagons at Vulcan sidings ready for despatch to the Docks; the platform could be slewed sideways to clear platform edges and tunnel restrictions. These loads were conveyed either at weekend or Sundays and often involved 'both lines occupation' during transit.

7728
BOX
2694

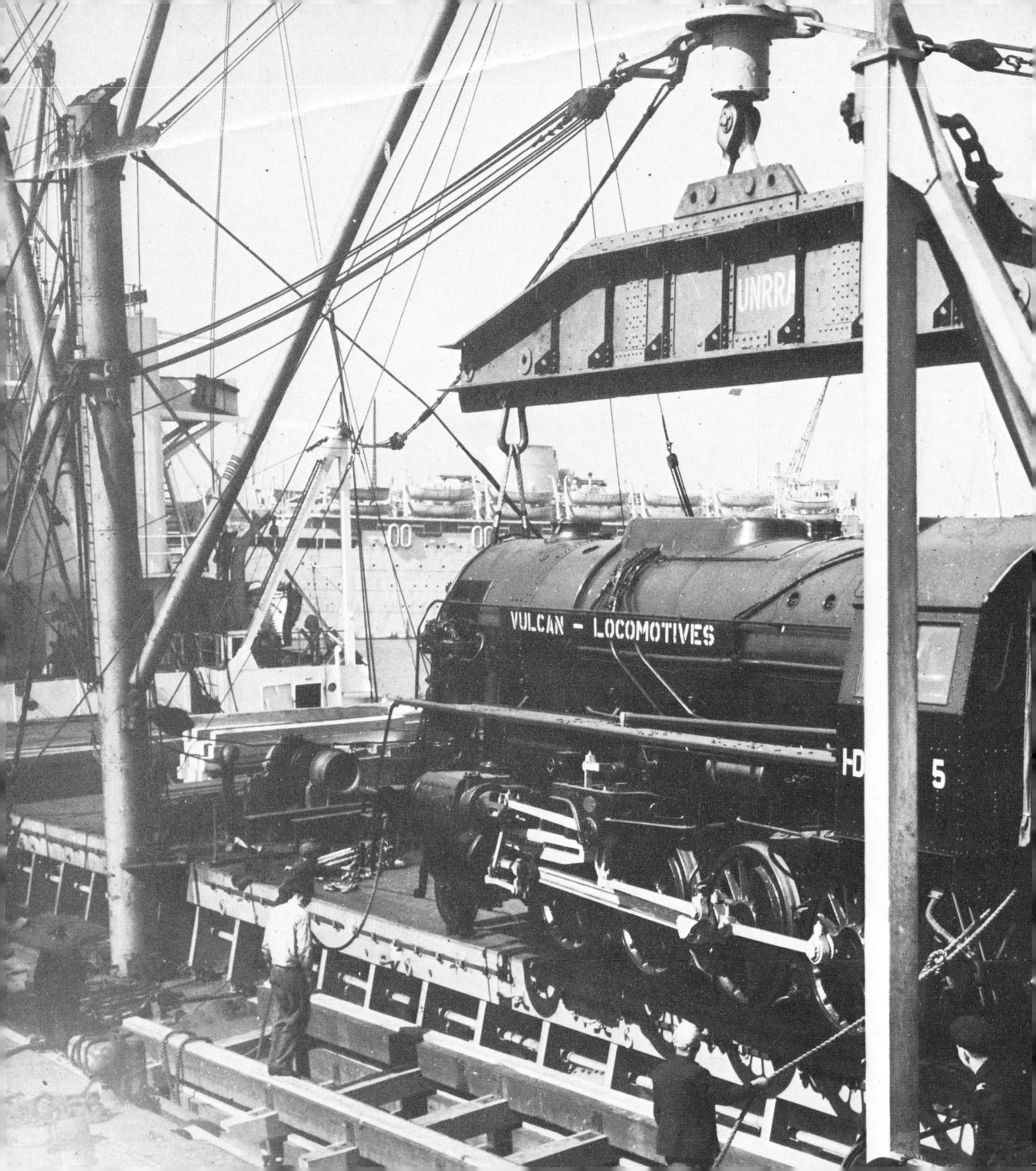
UNRRA
VULCAN - LOCOMOTIVES
5

A 'Liberation' 2-8-0 locomotive goes abroad; Birkenhead docks, 1946.

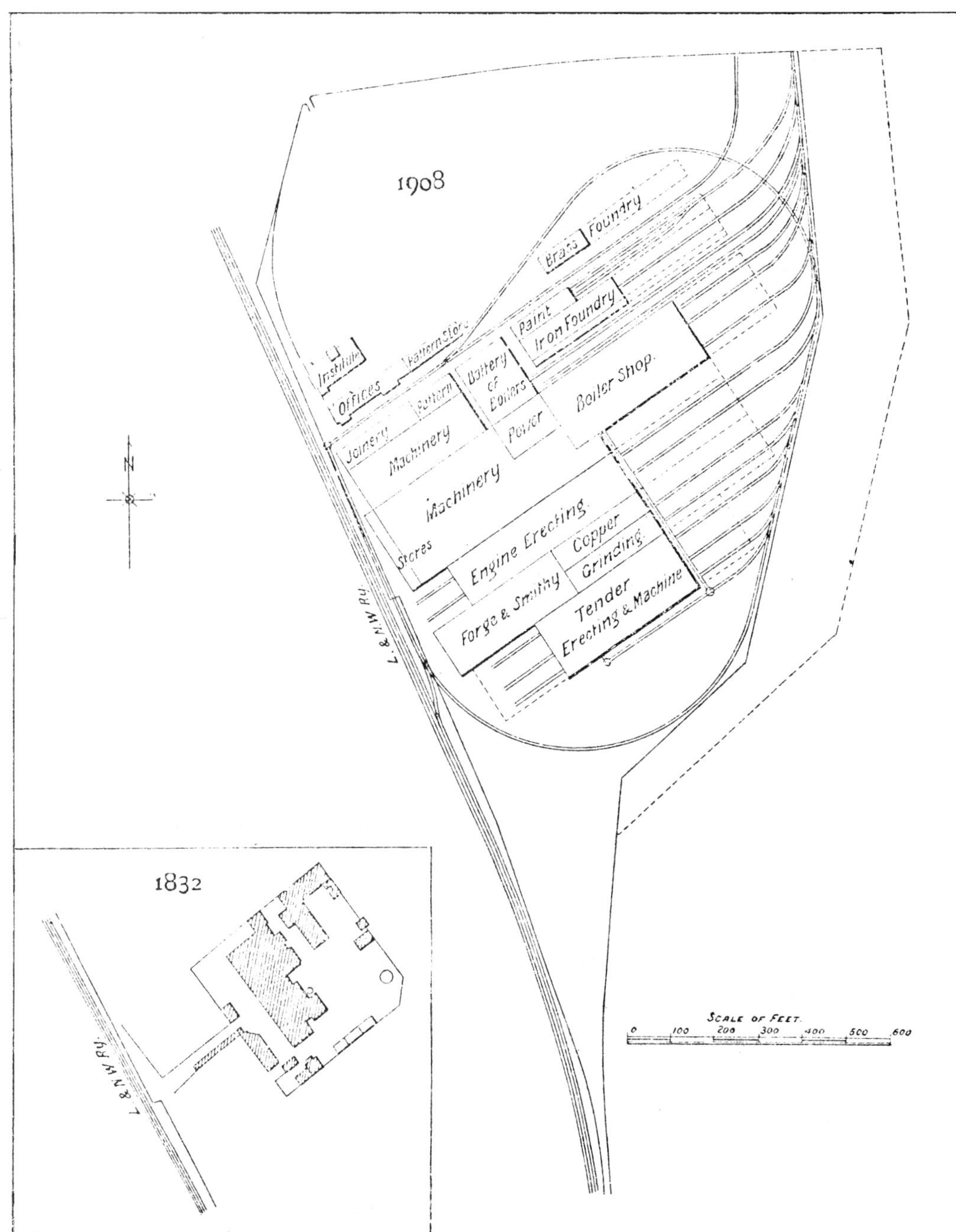

A plan of the Vulcan Foundry Works in 1908 (originally reproduced in *The Railway Gazette*) showing the general layout of the works, together with an inset plan, to the same scale, of the Works as it was in 1832.

A general view in the Erecting Shop showing a batch of 'XB' locomotives under construction for India. Note the heavy frame in the foreground, with its massive stays—essential on the sometimes mediocre tracks in India.

Two metre-gauge 'YD' 2-8-2 locomotives nearing completion, the nearer one being on the middle test track. This shop was equipped with two levels of crane tracks, this facility of high and low level cranes of 50-ton capacity permitting valuable flexibility in working.

A close up of one of the 'XB' Pacifics nearing completion. It is being prepared for valve setting; the next move will then be final wheeling, adding the bogies and truck, and then through the door to the testing road, which consisted of about a quarter of a mile of mixed gauge (3ft. 6in., 4ft. 8½in. and 5ft. 6in.) track.

Before the advent of road transport using specially designed vehicles in 1931, locomotives had to be unwheeled and broken down for rail transit to the docks. The 'XB' locomotive shown here has been unwheeled and is being conveyed to the paint shop after testing.

Another general view of the Erecting Shop with a further batch of 'XB's. In the left foreground is a newly delivered boiler from the Boiler department; this will be lifted on to the main frames behind.

A 'XB' Class boiler ready for steam test before fitting to the locomotive fram Testing was by hydraulic pressure, using hot water at a pressure 25 per cent in exc of normal working, followed by a steam test at normal pressure; this was continu for two hours. Note the large number of flexible stay cups on the firebox, which w the usual trouble spots if any difficulties occurred.

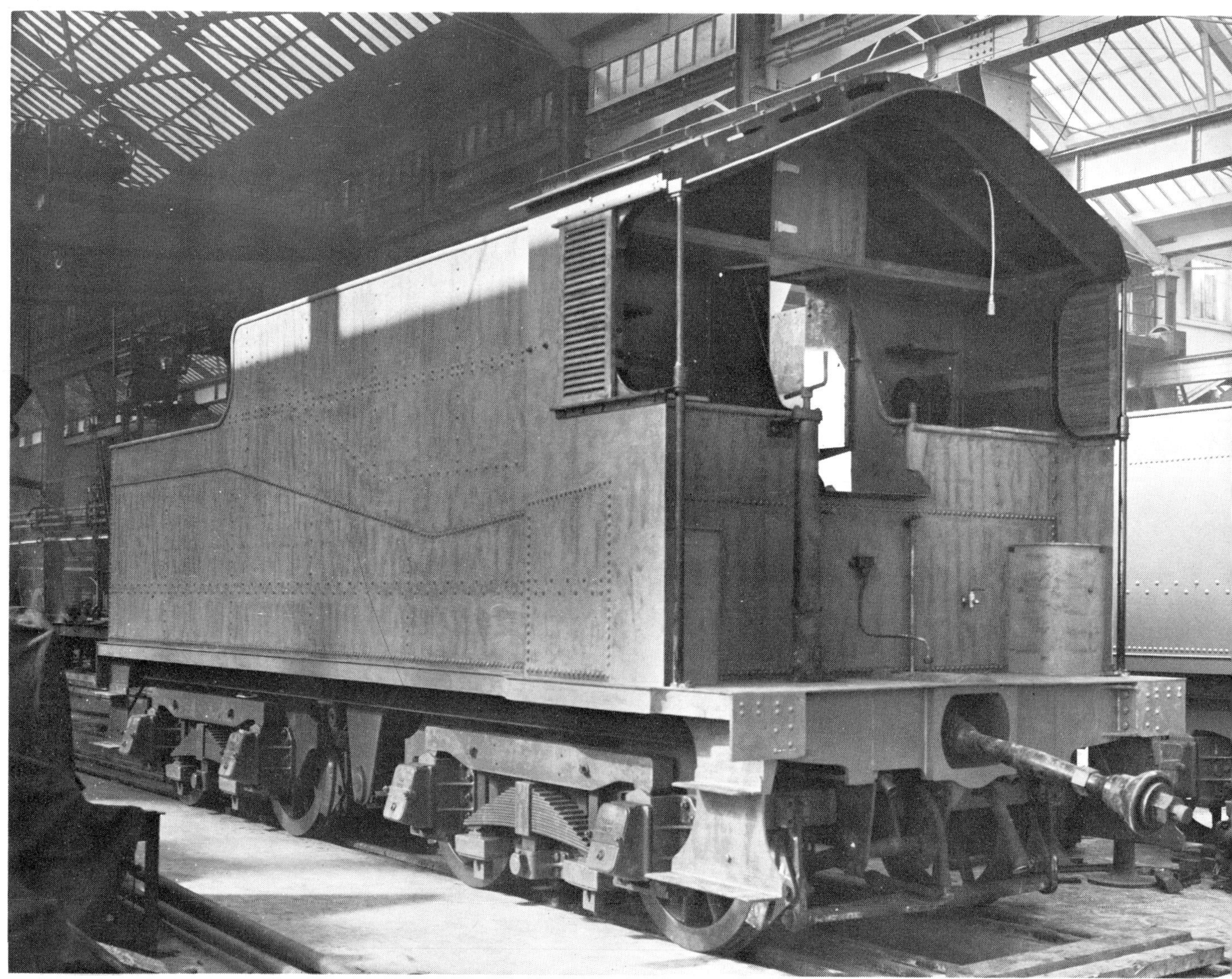

The standard Indian Railway broad gauge tender was fitted to all 'X' class locomotives. Teak shutters matching the locomotive cab and louvred cab roof with electric lighting were a feature. A patent draw-bar is shown. Capacity was 10 tons of coal, and 4,500 gallons of water.

A steel boiler shell and copper firebox for one of the Indian State Railway 'X' Class passenger 4-6-2s. In varying dimensions, this was a standard design for all the 'X' Classes and was a successful steam producer, using the low-grade Indian fuel.

A general view of a 'YD' locomotive under construction. These strong and simple machines were built by the hundred as a standard design, this particular batch being for the Assam Bengal Railway. Many are still running today in India and Burma.

A view of the three head Frame Slotting Machine built in 1912. Frame plates were cut out by oxy-acetelyne burning machines and with the early application of this method, the semi-rough finish was completely machined to avoid incipient stress cracks developing. Frames were usually of $1\frac{1}{4}$in.-$1\frac{3}{4}$in. thickness and later in 1945 3in. bar frames were adopted, and with the improvement in oxy-cutting practice, only the datum edges, i.e., horn gaps, top edge, etc., had to be machined. This machine was usually operated by two men and regularly double shifted. It had a bedplate of 90ft. in length and could machine two settings of main locomotive frames, each of fourteen inch depth, simultaneously. It was completely rebuilt and modernised in 1946 and continued to slot bar frames for the Indian Railways' new locomotive factory at Chitteranjan until 1958.

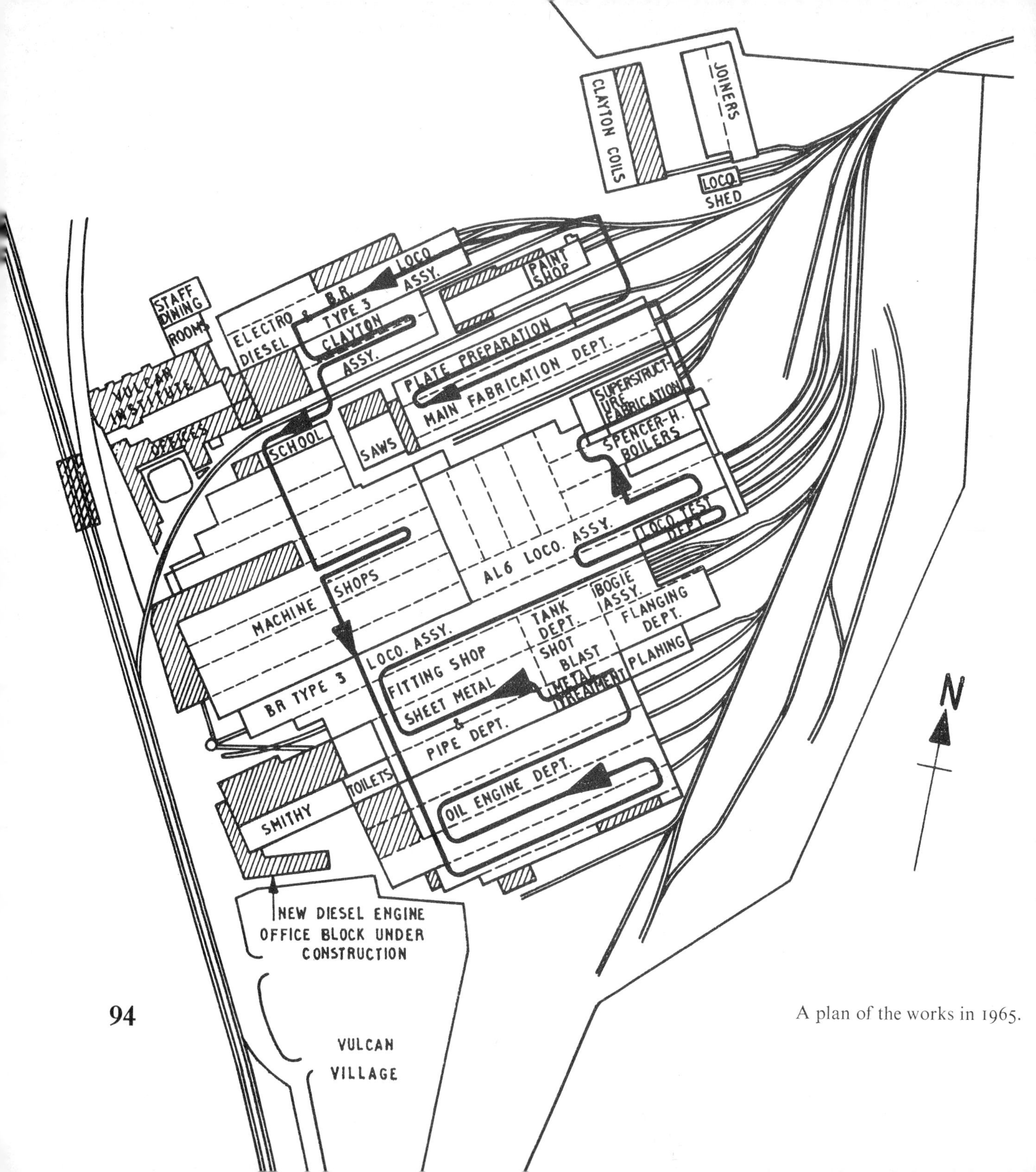

A plan of the works in 1965.

A 'double' event: steaming trials of two of the Experimental Pacifics constructed in 1930. These, the only four-cylinder Pacifics to run in India, were fitted with Lentz and Caprotti valve gears (see page 49). The right hand locomotive is complete and ready for the official photograph whilst that on the left is in normal steam test conditions with 'all covers off' for final adjustments. The works capacity was two to three locomotives per week. Right, a view of the early paint spray booth introduced in 1936. The shop is occupied by Buenos Ayres Great Southern tank locomotives preparing for shipment.

Steaming trials for one of the Nigerian Railway 4-8-2 locomotives in 1930, described on page 50. The foremen at that date were still bowler hatted, as were their contemporaries in the main railway shops.

INDEX

Works views 1920, 1947 7
Camden & Woodbury (USA) 1833 . . . 8
South Carolina Railway (USA) 1835 . . . 9
Liverpool & Manchester Rly. 0-4-0 (1834) . . 9
London & Greenwich Railway (1836) . . 10
North Union Railway 0-4-2 (1836) . . . 10
Great Western Railway 2-2-2 (1837) . . . 11
London & Birmingham Rly. (1838) . . . 11
Bristol & Birmingham Rly. 4-2-0 (1845) . . 12
Shrewsbury & Chester Railway (1848) . . . 12
Shrewsbury & Hereford Rly. (1853) . . . 12
Gt. Indian Peninsula Rly. (1852) . . . 13
Somerset & Dorset Rly. 2-4-0 (1866) . . . 14
Midland Rly. Kirtley 0-6-0 (1869) . . . 15
Japanese 3ft. 6in. 2-4-0 (1870) 16
New Zealand Railways Fairlie (1872) . . 16
Russo Konstantinofskoi Rly. (1871) . . . 17
London, Chatham & D. Rly. 0-4-4T (1875) . . 18
Ffestiniog Rly. 0-4-4T Fairlie (1876) . . . 18
Welsh Highland Rly. Fairlie (1875) . . . 19
Indian Railway 'F' Class 0-6-0 20
Indian Railway 'O' Class 4-4-0 . . . 20
Gt. Indian Peninsula Rly. 0-8-0T (1891) . . 21
Taff Vale Railway 4-4-2T (1888) . . . 22
Hull & Barnsley Rly. 0-6-0 (1891) . . . 22
Great Northern Rly. 4-4-0 compound . . 23
Buenos Ayres G.S.R. 4-6-0 compound . . 24
Burma Rlys 0-6-6-0 Fairlie (1907) . . . 25
Bombay, B. & C. India Railway 4-6-0 . . . 26
North Western Railway 0-6-0 (1908) . . . 27
East Indian Railway 4-4-2 (1908) . . . 27
Indian broad gauge 'H' Class 2-8-0 . . . 29
Indian broad gauge 'HG' Class 2-8-0 . . . 30
Madras & Southern Mahratta Rly. 4-4-0 . . 31
Eastern Bengal Rly. 4-6-0 (1910) . . . 31
Mexican Railways 0-6-6-0 Fairlie (1911) . . 32
Gt. Indian Peninsula Rly. 4-4-0 (1911) . . 33
East Indian Railway 2-6-4T (1912) . . . 34
Central Uruguay Rly. 4-4-4T (1915) . . . 35
French Artillery Department 2-8-0 (1917) . . 37
Gt. Indian Peninsula Rly. 'HP' Class 4-6-0 . . 38
Great Central Railway 4-6-0 (1921) . . . 38
L M S R Standard 0-6-0T (1922) . . . 39
Ceylon Govt. Railways 4-6-0 (1922) . . . 40
Gold Coast Rly. long-boilered 4-8-2 (1924) . . 41-2
Buenos Ayres Gt. Southern 2-6-4T (1925) . . 42
Indian railways 'YD' Class 2-8-2 43
Nigerian Railways 2-8-2 (1925) 44
L M S R compound 4-4-0 (1925) 45
Indian State Rlys. 'XD' Class 2-8-2 46
Indian State Rlys. 'XB' Class 4-6-2 46
Indian State Rlys. 'XC' Class 4-6-2 46
Indian State Rlys. 'XE' Class 2-8-2 47
Indian State Rlys. 'XA' Class 4-6-2 47
Indian State Rlys. 'YC' Class 4-6-2 47
Indian State Rlys. 'YB' Class 4-6-2 48
Indian State Rlys. experimental Pacifics . . 49
Gt. Indian Peninsula Rly. 2600hp electrics . . 49
Nigerian Rlys. 3-cylinder 4-8-2 (1930) . . . 50
L M S R Stanier Class 5 4-6-0 51
Buenos Ayres Gt. Southern 4-6-2 (1938) . . 53-4
Chinese National Rlys. 4-8-4 (1936) . . . 55-6
Indian railways 'W' Class 2-6-4T 58
Indian railways 'WW' Class 0-6-2T 58
East Indian Railway 2-4-2T (1940) 59
'Austerity' 2-8-0 (1943-5) 60-1
'Liberation' 2-8-0 (post-war) 62-3
East Indian Railway 'HP/S' 4-6-0 (1946) . . 64
Nigerian Railways 2-8-2 'River' Class . . . 65
LNER 'B1' Class 4-6-0 65
Turkish State Railways 2-10-0 (1948) . . . 66
Central Argentine Railways 4-6-2 68
Tasmanian Railways 4-8-2 (1950) 68
Queensland Railways (Australia) 4-6-2 . . . 69
Indian Govt. Rlys. 'WG' Class 2-8-2 . . . 69
Egyptian State Railways 2-8-0 (1952) . . . 70
East African Railways 2-8-2 (1952) . . . 70
Victoria Railways 'K' Class 2-8-0 71
North Borneo Rlys. 'Austerity' 2-6-2 (1956) . . 72
Antofagasta (Bolivia) Rly. 4-8-2 74
Persian railways 'Santa Fe' 2-10-2 75
East African Railways 2-8-4 (1955) . . . 76
Indian railways lightweight Pacific . . . 76
L M Region Class 5 No. 45110 77
Vulcan Works steam shunter 78
Indian Govt. Railways 'HPS' Class 80
'Liberation' Class 2-8-0 82
Vulcan Foundry, plan of the Works (1908) . . 84
Interior views 85-93
Vulcan Foundry, plan of the Works (1965) . . 94
Steaming trials of experimental Pacifics . . . 95
Steaming trials of Nigerian 4-8-2 95